The Practical Guide to
# WINE

# The Practical Guide to
# WINE

*Ann and Terence Pierce*

PRACTICAL PUBLISHING CORPORATION

Copyright 1983 Ann and Terence Pierce. All rights reserved.

Published by The Practical Publishing Corporation,
P. O. Box 1020, Lenox Hill Station
New York, NY 10021

Printed in the United States of America.

LC 83-63078

Special thanks go to Patricia Bernblum, who designed this book, and whose help and advice were invaluable in making it all possible.

# Contents

1. *Introduction*  7

2. *Types of Wine*  11
   Where to Start; How Wines are Named; Types of Wine; How Wine is Made; The Importance of the Grape Varietal; Famous Wines and Their Grapes

3. *How to Store and Serve Wine*  27
   How to Store Wine; Vintages; Wine and Food; Serving Temperatures; Glasses; Opening the Wine; Decanting Wines; Wine as Alcohol; Serving Wine

4. *How to Buy Wine*  45
   Buying Wine; Investing in Wine; Wine for Weddings and Parties; Ordering Wine in a Restaurant; Wine Labeling Laws in the United States; Label Information

5. *What to Look for in Wine*  59
   Procedure; Evaluation

6. *A Step by Step Approach to Wine Appreciation*  73
   Look, Listen and Learn; Try, Taste and Test; Relish, Remember and Write; Wine Appreciation Card; Wine Appreciation Course

7. *Quality Considerations — The French Example*  87
   How Much Are Wine Labeling Laws Really Worth?; Government Quality Classifications

8.  **The Wines of Bordeaux      95**
    Introduction; Grape Varietals; Vintages; Appellation Contrôlée Classifications; The Producer; The Importer; How to Select a Bordeaux; Bordeaux Districts and Communes

9.  **The Wines of Burgundy      107**
    Introduction; Grape Varietals; Vintages; Appellation Contrôlée Classifications; The Producer; The Importer; How to Select a Burgundy; Burgundy Communes

10. **The Wines of Champagne and Other French Wines      119**
    Champagne; Introduction; Grape Varietals; Vintages; Appellation Contrôlée Classifications; La Méthode Champenoise (the Champagne Method); The Producer; Other French Wines; The Wines of Alsace; Wines from the Loire Valley; Wines from the Rhône Valley

11. **The Wines of Germany      131**
    Introduction; Official Classifications; The Producer; The Importer; The Grape Varietals; The Vintage; Designations of Origin; The Winemaking Regions of Germany

12. **The Wines of Italy      143**
    Introduction; Official Classifications; Producers and Importers; Vintages; The Winemaking Regions of Italy

13. **The Wines of the United States      155**
    Introduction; Official Classifications; Grape Varietals; The Producer; The Wines of New York State; The Wines of California; Vintages

    *Index      167*

# 1. Introduction

Wine is to be enjoyed, nothing more and nothing less. The purpose of this book is to give you the knowledge and the confidence to buy the wines that you will enjoy and to avoid those that should be left on the shelf. It will help you to select, buy, evaluate, store, and serve wine for any occasion.

Most wine books seem to be written for people who already have some knowledge of the subject. This one is different, and assumes no knowledge on the part of the reader. At the same time, it has been designed to be of practical value to all wine consumers, regardless of their level of expertise.

It provides a detailed course that you can follow in your own home, at your own speed. This course was structured so that you can start at the beginning, if you have had little experience in the different types of wine, or anywhere in the middle.

We not only cover good wines, but also how to recognize the things that can go wrong with a wine. As a result, you will be able to identify a bad bottle in a restaurant or elsewhere and send it back with confidence for a refund!

We suggest how to store and serve wine, using procedures that are absolutely correct in any social situation—formal or informal. We cover corkscrews and how to open wine bottles, what type of glasses to use, when to decant wine and the correct wines to serve with meals. Since these procedures are used to make the wine taste its best, they are just as appropriate in your home as in the most elegant French château, and they need not be expensive.

There is a special section on buying wines in a restaurant. We show you how to order and taste the wine using procedures that will establish you as an expert in the eyes of the wine waiter (called the "sommelier" in expensive restaurants). This will put you, not the waiter, in command of the situation.

In addition, we discuss the wine labeling laws in the United States and in the other major winemaking countries. You will thus learn what the terms on the label really mean to you as a consumer.

Finally, we describe the major wines of France, Germany, Italy and the United States in some detail so that you should have a reasonably good idea of what to expect when you purchase a wine from any of these countries.

There are only a few facts that you really need to learn, and a few simple rules to follow. In places, we may have oversimplified some of the more complex subjects, but nothing of importance has been omitted.

We believe strongly that the enjoyment of wine is strictly a matter of personal taste, and that you should always follow your own judgment, regardless of what anyone else says.

We go into enough detail so that you can develop confidence in your judgment in any surroundings. We also show you how to use each wine that you taste as a building block to increase your expertise.

Although there are many factors that the wine professional has to consider, there are really only four major considerations for the normal consumer.

Does the wine have a pleasant scent? Does it have an agreeable taste? How good is the aftertaste left on the tongue and palate after the wine has been swallowed? Is it good value for the money?

The scent of the wine is usually called the "aroma," or the "bouquet"—pronounced boo-kay. The aftertaste is normally referred to as the "finish."

In summary, the aroma of the wine should be clean and fresh, and should have the characteristics of the type of grape (called the grape "varietal") from which the wine was made.

The taste of the wine should be slightly fruity, with no bitterness and no taste of vinegar. It should be slightly acidic, to make it refreshing, but not excessively so. It should rarely be noticeably sweet.

Once the wine has been swallowed, the finish should be smooth and pleasant, but not overpowering. The price should reflect the quality of the wine.

This is not to say that each wine does not have its own character, for it does. This character will differ, depending on the type of wine. A powerful, full-bodied red wine should be quite different from a dry white wine. The degree to which a particular wine shows the characteristics expected of it is an important indication of its quality. We give you the characteristics to look for in each wine covered.

We usually use the word "producer" for the firm or individual responsible for making the wine, blending it, bottling it and bringing it to market. We do not mention any producer or make of wine by name, since the purpose of this book is to help you with all wines, not just those we happen to like.

We wish you luck as you explore the variety of wines available to you. We have based this book on many years of experience, in many places; by following the advice given, you should learn how to find excellent wines at very good prices.

We have no vested interest in seeing you buy any particular wine, or any wine at all, for that matter. Our interest is to give you enough knowledge and confidence to buy and serve wine anywhere, any time, and in any company.

# 2. Types of Wine

The purpose of this chapter is to provide a guide to the types of wines that are available, and to help you select those types that you are likely to enjoy. There is also a brief description of how different types of wine are made in order to help you to appreciate the differences between the various wines on the market.

## *Where to Start*

There seems to be a bewildering array of bottles, countries, varietals, colors, regions and much more, to choose from. However, it is not as complicated as it may seem at first sight. In reality, when you buy a wine, just as when you buy a car, there are only a few major categories to choose from, with a number of "options" that make the wine more or less desirable to you.

Of course, just as for automobiles, there are many exotic wines (or makes of car) that cater to the experienced enthusiast. We do mention some of the Rolls Royces and Ferraris of the wine world, because they are interesting and discussed often in the wine literature.

The main purpose of this book is to get you comfortable with the wine equivalents of the Fords, Toyotas and Buicks that you are likely to come across on a daily basis. We also want to make sure that you get a Mercedes, if you are paying for one.

In the automobile business there are a dozen major manufacturers around the world, and a couple of dozen smaller companies. Each of the major manufacturers produces a number of different models which are designed to appeal to different people.

A similar situation exists for wine, where there are only a half dozen major categories. The wines within each category are similar in terms of what you should expect of the wine, how it should be served, and the foods that accompany it well. The major differences between the categories depend on the color of the wine, and whether it is sweet or dry, still or sparkling. Within each category are specific types of wine, which are made from different grape varietals, and which may be considered as different models.

## How Wines are Named

A good place to start is by looking at the names given to wines, and how you can use this information to help you. The name of a wine consists of two parts: the type of wine, and the name of the firm that made it (the producer).

*The Type of Wine*   The way a wine will taste depends on the grape varietals used and the winemaking methods employed to make the wine. The name of the type of wine will tell you both of these.

Most of the better European wines are named after the place where the wine was made, called the "Designation of Origin" (e.g. Bordeaux, Champagne, Chianti, Burgundy etc.). The name given to a designated winemaking region (and to the wine) may refer to a specific town in the area, a small village, a river, or even be the name specifically given to the winegrowing region. Unless you are interested in geography, it is only important to try to remember the type of wine from the region.

The regulations define which grape varietals and winemaking methods may be used to make the wine before a particular Designation of Origin may be used. You thus know a good deal about any wine using one.

For example, when you buy a red French Burgundy, you know that the wine is a full-bodied red wine, made from Pinot Noir grapes grown in the officially defined Burgundy region of France. The requirements for all of the major wines are described farther on in this book.

The better American wines are named after the type of grape used in making the wine (e.g. Pinot Noir, Sauvignon Blanc). Thus, when you buy an American Sauvignon Blanc, you know that the wine will be a dry white wine, similar to the white wines of Bordeaux.

*The Name of the Producer* The label also shows the name of the producer of the wine. For the less expensive jug wines, where the legal requirements for superior wines have not been met, this is all you will find to guide you about the the quality of the wine. Some producers usually make good wines, others are not so good.

Some producers only produce wines from a single estate, in which case the wine is generally named after the estate (usually with the specific "Estate Bottled" wording described farther on in this book).

Others produce and/or market wines from several estates. When these comply with the legal requirements for superior wines, they will also carry the prestigious Designation of Origin described above.

## Types of Wine

Wine is made from the juice of ripe grapes which has fermented naturally. It can be red, white or rosé (pink), and may be sparkling (with bubbles as in Champagne) or still (no bubbles).

It is usually dry, but may occasionally be sweet if some sugar is left (or added) after fermentation has ended (when talking about wine, dry is the opposite of sweet, not the opposite of wet).

Depending on the type of wine, the alcohol content ranges between 8% by volume to around 16%. It is normally around 10%. Depending on many factors, prices can range from a few dollars to many hundreds of dollars per bottle.

The table at the end of this chapter can be used as a catalog of the major wines of the world that you need to be concerned with (except for Fortified Wines, which are outside the scope of this book). It shows the major categories of wines (full-bodied red, dry white etc.), the most famous types of wine within each one, (Bordeaux, Chablis etc.), and the grape varietals usually used to make that type of wine (Cabernet Sauvignon, Chardonnay etc.).

The following paragraphs describe the important characteristics of each category in more detail.

*Full-Bodied Red Wines* (Examples: French Burgundy, American Cabernet Sauvignon, Italian Barolo). These are the kings of the red wine family. They are usually made primarily from a single, strong tasting grape varietal which imparts a forceful character to the wine. Sometimes, the producer will blend in a small amount of a milder grape, with less tannin in the skin, to soften the taste.

The color of the wine tends to be a darker red than that of the lighter red wines. The taste and the aroma tend to be fuller and more complex, which is why we classify these wines as "full-bodied". Furthermore, they tend to be more temperamental, and spoil rapidly if they are stored improperly for a period of more than a very few months.

Full-bodied red wines should be dry to the taste, with absolutely no indication of sweetness. They should have a strong, somewhat complex taste, which clearly shows the character of the varietal from which the wine was made. The finish, which is particularly important for these wines, should be powerful, long lasting, and with no bitterness.

When young, these wines tend to be somewhat sharp until the aging process in the bottle has caused the tannins to break down, and the wine to become more mellow. To drink them at their best, they should be kept for several years under proper storage conditions. The vintage is important, and wines from the better vintages will last longer than those from the poorer vintages.

However, since few of us can afford to hold wines for several years, they can, and usually are, drunk much younger, and there is nothing wrong with this. In Chapter 3, we discuss the decanting of full-bodied red wines and the reasons why this improves a young full-bodied red wine.

Good full-bodied red wines are temperamental, complex, and in short supply. They thus tend to be rather expensive. As a result, many people only try one or two. Since they don't know what they are doing, they do not decant the wine, and they often buy them in a restaurant where the wine has not been properly stored. As a result they are disappointed with the results and often do not try again.

However, these are also the finest red wines made, and those that are the most often talked and written about. The result is that many consumers know that they ought to like these wines, but are afraid to try them again. Do not be dismayed! There are some fine full-bodied red wines around, and one of the purposes of this book is to help you to find good ones, without having to pay a fortune for them.

*Light Red Wines* (Examples: French Beaujolais, most blended jug wines, Italian Bardolino and Valpolicella). These are lighter than the full-bodied red wines in the taste as well as in the power and complexity of the aroma. They should always have a fresh, fruity aroma, which will never be as powerful as that of the full-bodied wines. They should be drunk young (1 - 4 years, at most).

These wines should never have a noticeably sharp taste, apart from the minimum acidity necessary for all wines to make them interesting. The finish should be fresh and not last too long in the mouth.

Even the best of them is seldom very expensive, and it is rare to find one in poor condition, unless it is too old, or has been stored very badly indeed. Since these wines are also uncomplicated and refreshing, they are often the best red wines to start experimenting with.

*Dry White Wines* (Examples: French white Burgundy, American Chardonnay, Italian Soave, most German Rhine and Mosel wines). White wines are not really white at all, but range from a light straw to a deep golden color, sometimes with a tinge of green. The term "white" is used to describe any wine without any pigmentation from red or purple grape skins.

White wine is usually made from white (actually green) grapes, but some fine white wines are also made from the juice of red grapes. Champagne, for example, is often made from the same Pinot Noir grape as the famous red wines of Burgundy.

Dry white wines generally have an uncomplicated fruity aroma and taste, both of which should indicate clearly the character of the grape varietal. Most of these wines should be drunk within about four years of the harvest; some of the better ones improve for a few more years.

You will sometimes see white wines marketed with the words Blanc de Blancs, which is French for "white (wine) from white (grapes)". This is often assumed to be something desirable, an indication of quality. It is nothing of the kind, and merely means that the wine was made from white grapes!

*Sweet White Wines* (Examples: "pop" wines, French Sauternes, German Auslese and other late-picked wines). There are two types of sweet wines, those that have been artificially sweetened, and those that are naturally sweet.

All inexpensive sweet wines have been artificially sweetened and are usually referred to as "pop" wines. It is not generally appropriate to serve them with food, since the sugar in the wine depresses the appetite. These sweet wines receive few compliments from these who know their wines and are often described as "alcoholic colas" used to wean the consumer from soft drinks. However, as we have said before, your own personal taste is the most important factor for choosing and enjoying wine.

The other type of sweet wines, however, rank among the most majestic, and, unfortunately, among the most expensive of all wines made today. These are the powerful dessert wines of the Sauternes (and Barsac) communes of the Bordeaux area of France, and the Rhine and Mosel areas of Germany.

These wines, described more fully in the chapters on wines from Bordeaux and Germany, should be a golden color, with a very powerful aroma, a fruity and somewhat sweet taste, and a long, powerful, smooth finish.

These are the only white wines that have sufficient character to age well in the bottle. Ideally, they should be drunk after they are 10 years old. They are also delicious when young.

*Rosé Wines* (Examples: French Rosé d'Anjou, American Grenache, Portuguese Rosé). The better rosé wines are made from red grapes, and the skins are removed from the grape juice before too much of the red pigmentation has passed from the skins to the wine. Some lesser rosé wines, generally those that do not carry any of the legal quality classifications, are made by blending red wine with white wine.

The color should range from a light pink with a hint of gold to a darker pink with a touch of purple. It should not be amber, or have a marked brownish color, both of which are danger signals that the wine may be too old.

The aroma and taste should be light, fruity, dry and refreshing. The finish should also be pleasant and dry, without any sharpness or bitterness. It should not last very long in the mouth.

Because these wines have little tannin, they should be drunk before they are three or four years old. The differences in quality between different vintages is rarely significant.

The nice thing about rosé wines is that few of them are very expensive, even the best of them. Furthermore, since they are not complex, and are drunk young, it is rare to have a truly bad experience with a rosé wine. For this reason, many people start their wine drinking experience with rosé wines.

*Sparkling Wines* (Examples: French or American Champagne, German Sekt, Italian Asti Spumanti). Sparkling wines are made so that a significant amount of carbon dioxide is in the wine when it is sold. The cork should come out with a satisfying pop, and there should be lots of bubbles in the wine when it is poured and drunk.

They are usually white, although some excellent sparkling rosé wines are made, and even some red ones, although the latter are generally undistinguished. The color of the white wines should range from a pale straw to an amber color.

The best sparkling wines are usually dry, although many producers also produce relatively sweet wines (Asti Spumanti is usually rather sweet). The taste and the aroma should be fruity and fresh, and the finish should be light, with no bitterness, and will generally not last for long. Sparkling wines should be drunk young (four to five years old).

The carbon dioxide may be in the bottle as a result of fermentation taking place in the bottle after it has been sealed so that the gas cannot escape until the bottle is opened at your table. This is the so called *Méthode Champenoise* (French for Champagne Method), which is described in the chapter on French Champagne.

Alternatively, the wine is allowed to ferment in the normal way and is then bottled under considerable pressure of carbon dioxide. This is often referred to as the "Tank Method".

It is fashionable to say that the Champagne method is the only way to go, and you will often see sparkling wines marketed with considerable emphasis on the fact that this was the method used. We feel that the method used is considerably less important than the quality of the wine to begin with, although most producers of high quality sparkling wines generally use the Champagne method.

Sparkling wines always have a mushroom shaped cork, which can be gripped outside of the bottle, and a wire cage to hold the cork in place until the bottle is opened.

*Fortified Wines*   These are the higher alcohol wines, that are usually sweet and often flavored using secret recipes of herbs or spices. They are called "fortified" because additional alcohol has been added to the wine, to make it stronger than it would be naturally.

Any wine whose alcohol content is above 16% alcohol

by volume is, by definition, a fortified wine. Examples are wines such as Port, Sherry, Vermouths and the proprietary Apéritif wines, mainly from France and Italy.

## How Wine is Made

Wine can be made from many different fruit (e.g. Peach Wine, made from peaches). When the word "wine" is used without the addition of another fruit in the name, it means that the liquid was produced entirely from grape juice.

Although each producer uses his own special techniques, the basic principles are the same for all wines. Any significant differences used for the various wine types are discussed farther on in this book when the particular wine is being described.

After the grapes have ripened, they are harvested and are crushed in a clean container. The natural yeast on the skins reacts with the sugar in the juice to produce alcohol and carbon dioxide gas (which is usually allowed to escape into the air). This natural process is called "fermentation".

At some point, depending on the type of wine desired, the fermenting grape juice (called "must") is separated from the solid matter, consisting of the pulp, skins, pits and stems. The fermentation is allowed to continue until all the sugar has been converted to alcohol. Other changes also take place, and the liquid becomes a wine, rather than an alcoholic grape juice.

Thus, the riper the grapes, the more sugar will be in the grape juice, and the stronger and better will be the wine. If the grapes are not sufficiently sweet, some sugar is sometimes added to the must before fermentation. This will enable the wine to reach the minimum required alcohol content.

This addition of sugar is called "chaptalization". Although it is not considered desirable for the finest wines, it is sometimes necessary. It is generally not possible to detect chaptalization when reading the label or even when tasting the wine.

Once the fermentation has been completed, the wine is clarified (called "fining") to remove any remaining solid matter. It is then stabilized, usually by the use of sulfur dioxide or another sulfur based chemical. Almost all of the sulfur dioxide passes through the wine, and it is usually indetectable. However, some producers use other sulfite chemicals for this purpose, and some people are allergic to sulfite chemicals.

If you suffer from this allergy, we probably do not have to tell you to be careful of the wines you drink. Under present law, winemakers do not have to tell the consumer which specific chemicals are used.

After the wine has been stabilized, it is aged for some time in the vats in which the wine fermented, or in wooden barrels where full-bodied red wines pick up some flavor from the wood. This aging period may vary from a few hours to several years, depending on the type of wine.

Each producer selects the aging period for his wines. White, rosé and light red wines will generally be aged for a very short period, while the more robust full-bodied red wines will be aged "in the wood" for two or more years.

Once the wine has been aged for the appropriate time, it is ready for bottling. Sometimes, all of the wine in a particular bottle will come from grapes grown on a single estate, in which case the label will show the wine to be "Estate Bottled". These are usually premium wines.

Most wines, however, are blends of several wines from different batches of grapes and may include wines from different grape varietals. The exact blend will be regulated for wines sold under a specific Designation of Origin. Otherwise, the producer will blend the wines to produce the type of wine that he is trying to make.

The bottle is labeled and it is then sealed, usually with a cork and a lead foil or plastic covering over the mouth of the bottle. The wine is now ready for sale and can be drunk.

Sometimes, the wine will be pasteurized or otherwise treated before being bottled. This process is performed to prevent any further changes from taking place in the bottle.

Since the effects of bottle aging are generally desirable for premium wines, most pasteurized wines are of lower quality. Although the label will not tell you that the wine has been pasteurized, a good rule of thumb is that these wines are usually sealed with a metal cap, rather than with a cork.

Some wine producers like to produce a wine that is distinctly sweet. Under normal conditions, the yeasts in the wine will ferment all of the available sugar to make alcohol, in which case the wine will be dry, and not sweet!

To make a sweet wine, it is thus necessary to render the yeasts ineffective before fermentation is completed. This is also done by pasteurizing the wine, or by passing it through special filters that are so fine that the yeasts are left behind. The exceptions are the special wines from Sauternes and the Rhine, where a quirk of nature allows exceptional sweet wines to be produced naturally.

All inexpensive sweet table wines are made by adding sugar or unfermented grape juice to otherwise indifferent wines which have been treated to stop the fermentation. These sweetened wines are generally white or rosé, and may be sparkling or still, although some sweet red wines can also be found.

Fortified wines are made by adding alcohol to the wine, usually before the fermentation process is completed. This addition of alcohol stops the fermentation, since the yeasts cannot function if the alcohol content is above about 16% by volume.

Thus, fortified wines can retain some of the natural sweetness of the grape juice when the distilled alcohol is added before all of the sugar has been converted to alcohol. The additional ingredients may be added to the wine while fermentation is taking place, or may be added afterwards.

## The Importance of the Grape Varietal

In the table at the end of this chapter, you will notice that we give a great deal of emphasis to the grape varietal. It thus seems appropriate at this time to discuss the role of the grape varietal.

The fact that the majority of these varietals are associated with European (mainly French) wines is by no means a question of snobbery or of bias on our part. The long history of winemaking in Europe has provided the opportunity to select and breed the grapes that make the finest wines in each winegrowing region. Historically, the French have set the standards by which all the world judges wine.

With the increasing investment in winemaking taking place in the United States, future editions of this book, written in 50 years, will probably have more United States varietals. In the meantime, most of the finest wines produced in the United States are made from European grape varietals.

If you like red wine from Bordeaux, it is very probable that you will also like other wines made from the Cabernet Sauvignon grape from the United States, Chile or anywhere else that this grape is grown.

Conversely, if you like a wine made from the Chardonnay grape, grown in California, you will almost certainly like a French white Burgundy or a French Chablis, both of which are also made from this grape in France, and which made it famous.

Any white wine that is made in France, and is labeled "Chablis" or "Burgundy" must, by law, be made from the Chardonnay grape, and any red French Bordeaux will be made primarily from one of the grapes in the Cabernet Sauvignon family.

Even though there are a large number of names to choose from in selecting a wine, all the major wines are made from just a few grape varietals. Once you have mastered these few, the rest is much easier. Furthermore, if you are only interested in one or two of the wines, full-bodied red wines and dry white wines, for example, you can ignore the others, and the list is even shorter!

## Famous Wines and Their Grapes

| Varietal | Type of wine | Country of Origin |
|---|---|---|
| **Full-Bodied Red Wines** | | |
| Cabernet Sauvignon | Bordeaux | France |
| Pinot Noir | Burgundy | France |
| Barbera | Barbera | Italy |
| Nebbiolo | Barbaresco/Barolo | Italy |
| Zinfandel | Zinfandel | U.S.A. |
| **Light Red Wines** | | |
| Gamay | Beaujolais | France |
| **Dry White Wines** | | |
| (Pinot) Chardonnay | Burgundy/Chablis | France |
| Sauvignon Blanc | Bordeaux; Loire | France |
| Semillon | Bordeaux | France |
| Chenin Blanc | Vouvray (Loire) | France |
| Riesling | Rhine/Mosel | Germany |
| **Sweet White Wines** | | |
| Semillon (late picked) | Sauternes | France |
| Riesling (late picked) | Rhine/Mosel | Germany |
| **Rosé Wines** | | |
| Grenache | Tavel (Rhône) | France |
| **Sparkling Wines** | | |
| Pinot Noir | Champagne | France |
| (Pinot) Chardonnay | Champagne | France |

# 3. How to Store and Serve Wine

This chapter covers how wine should be stored in order to keep it in good condition and how to serve it with elegance and style. We cover the types of wine to serve with meals, the importance of vintages, the temperature at which each wine should be served, the glasses to use, how to open a wine bottle and when you should decant wine. By following these suggestions, you can be perfectly confident in any social situation in which wine is to be served.

*How to Store Wine*

Wine is a living liquid. There are various harmless bacteria and other organisms in the bottle which react with the wine in the bottle and change its character.

This usually softens the somewhat sharp taste of the tannins, which come from the skins, pips and stems of the grapes (and the wood from the barrel when the wine was aged in the wood). Some of the natural acids in the wine are also neutralized.

If the wine is not particularly tannic to start with, this interraction is not desirable, since it makes the wine dull and rather flat. Most white wines, all rosé and all light red wines are not very tannic, and so they do not improve as they age in the bottle. Therefore, they should be drunk within a year or so of being made.

Full-bodied red wines are very sharp when young and improve by being allowed to mature for several years in the bottle before being drunk. The late-picked sweet wines of Sauternes and the Rhine also improve with age, as do some of the fortified wines, particularly Port and Madeira.

As these changes are taking place in the bottle, the wine is slowly producing a fine insoluble powder, known as the "sediment". While the sediment is harmless, it is unattractive and can also affect the taste of the wine.

Unfortunately, the process does not stop magically when the wine is fully mature. Even the most robust of these wines will eventually become flat, dull and then very bitter. When this happens, the wine is said to be "over the hill" and is no longer drinkable.

The conditions under which it is stored have a great effect on the wine. This can also have a serious impact on your pocket if you find, as we once did, that some very fine wine that is being saved for a special occasion has been ruined by improper storage. It then has to be replaced, several years later, at a much higher price.

The enemies of wine are temperature changes, oxygen, light, vibration, and very low humidity. Over the centuries, winemakers have found that the ideal storage conditions for wine are in deep underground cellars. The temperature is a relatively constant 50 - 60 degrees (Fahrenheit), it is dark, somewhat damp, and there is no vibration.

Wine is not very fussy about the actual temperature at which it is stored; this can be anywhere between about 45 and about 70 degrees. The warmer the temperature, the faster the wine will mature. If the temperature is much above 70 degrees, the maturing process is too rushed to be good for the wine.

More important is that the temperature not fluctuate by more than about 10 degrees. Excessive temperature variations seem to upset the wine, with the result that even the most robust full-bodied red wines are destroyed in less than a year.

If the wine storage area is too dry, the corks dry out, and additional air enters the bottle. The result is that the vinegar bacteria, which need the presence of oxygen to thrive, turn the wine to vinegar. However, the corks dry out rather slowly, provided that the bottle is stored on its side with the entire inside of the cork covered by the wine. If this is done, you can safely store wine in an area that is too dry for a few years.

Vinegar bacteria also become active as soon as the wine bottle is opened, and wine should normally be drunk within a few hours of opening the bottle. If you do not drink the whole bottle, it is sometimes possible to store the bottle overnight in the refrigerator. The wine should still be drinkable, if not as good, on the following day.

For reasons not fully understood, if the wine is subjected to continuous light, the changes in the wine are also rapid, unpredictable, and usually undesirable. The same is true for wines subjected to continuous vibration, although, in this case, the changes take place more slowly.

Wines stored in cellars on Park Avenue, in New York (too close to the New Haven Railroad), and over the subway systems in London and Paris have been found to deteriorate much faster than expected. Vibration was found to be the culprit.

If you are going to build a serious collection of wines, you should store it in an environment as close as possible to the conditions that exist in an underground cellar.

If you have a basement, so much the better, and you can put in an insulated closet against an outside wall away from any heating pipes. If the temperature still varies, you will need some air conditioning and possibly humidifying appliances as well.

If you do not have a basement, you will need to buy a special temperature-controlled wine storage unit. If you plan to get one of these, we recommend that you check the reliability carefully. We have one in our apartment, and it seems to break down every summer!

Without temperature-controlled surroundings, it is pointless to try to keep wine for a period of years in the hope that it will mature. If you do, you will surely find that when the time comes to drink the wine, it will be over the hill.

Nevertheless, it is always a good idea to have a bottle or two of wine available to serve to unexpected visitors. Must those people who live in apartments, or who do not have the correct storage conditions, only serve inexpensive, pasteurized jug wines to their unexpected guests?

There is clearly a compromise solution. With a little care, anyone can provide an environment that will keep fine wines in good condition for at least several months.

You should find a closet that is not hit by direct sunlight and is not opened every day. It should not be too close to a heating or cooling unit, so that the temperature is as constant as possible (even if it is too warm for optimal storage).

You should then get a wine rack, or some way of storing the wine on its side in such a way that you can take a bottle out from the bottom without disturbing the wines on the top. A good (and free!) example is an empty wine case which still has the cardboard dividers used to prevent the bottles from breaking in transit. Your friendly local wine store is usually only too happy to give these away.

Whenever you buy, or are given, a bottle of wine, just slip it in an empty compartment. If you buy a whole case of wine, we suggest that you simply open the top (without tearing it off), slip the whole case on its side in the closet, and take out the bottles one by one as you need them.

How long you can keep the wine depends on how close your closet is to the conditions described above. The key is to be conservative and not to try to keep the wine for too long.

## Vintages

A great deal is talked about vintages, and many people try to remember all sorts of dates when they are thinking about wine. We feel that the whole subject can be greatly simplified.

The first thing to remember is that vintages are only truly important for full-bodied red wines where the differences between two vintages can be the difference between a wine that is superb and one that is unpleasant to swallow. Early or late frosts, rain at the harvest time, a cool summer and not enough rain in the spring or summer are the primary problems that can have a devastating effect on the grapes, and thus on the wine.

If the weather is good (from the grapes' point of view!), the wine will be rich and complex and will last for several years. If the weather is poor, the tannins in the skin will not be fully developed, with the result that the wine will never be distinguished and will deteriorate rapidly.

The naturally sweet white wines can only be made in those years when the weather was favorable, so you do not have to be concerned with the quality of any particular vintage year for these wines.

For most other wines (rosé, dry white and red), the differences between even the best and the worst vintages is much less noticeable. A connoisseur will always be able to distinguish between vintages, but we feel that, for most people, these differences are too subtle to be truly significant.

Secondly, the differences between vintages are only truly significant in areas where the weather is very variable from year to year. Vintages are thus important for the full-bodied red wines of Bordeaux and Burgundy. The differences between good and bad years is less pronounced in the Rhône Valley of France, most of Italy and in California.

The vintage tables given in the sections on the wines from Bordeaux and Burgundy list the vintages since 1970 and give an indication of how the wines were to drink, as of early 1983. The numbers, from one to five, with five as the best, indicate the quality of the vintage as a whole.

All vintage tables including these, should be used with some caution. The use of a vintage chart is to improve your chances of getting a good wine. Although it is not guaranteed, a wine that was made in a good vintage year for a particular region should be better than one made in a poor year.

Individual wines may be better or worse than these averages. This is because the weather, in specific pockets of vineyards within the general area, may have been subtly different from that of the region as a whole.

Another reason is that a particular winemaker may have been smarter (or luckier) than his neighbors over the timing of the harvest. He may have waited longer than they did, with the result that his grapes were riper when they were picked. Alternatively, he may have waited too long, and the crop was damaged by rain or frost.

The vintage charts should also be used to tell you when these wines should ideally be drunk. Burgundies mature more quickly than the wines of Bordeaux; the best time to drink both of these wines is described in the chapters on each wine!

Even for white, rosé and sparkling wines, where the quality of the actual vintage is less important, it is helpful to know the year that a wine was made in order to make sure that you do not drink it too old! The finer white wines improve in the bottle for only a few years.

## Wine and Food

Many people are afraid of looking foolish by serving the "wrong" wine with food. There really is no need to be afraid, as this section will show. There are only two important things to remember.

The first is, as always, your own personal preference. If you, personally, prefer a full-bodied red wine with apple pie, a combination that is not often considered to be a happy one, there no reason for anyone to criticize you. They may not share your views, but so what?

The second is that the wine and the food should be allies rather than opponents, and one should not overpower the other. This means that light wines should accompany light, delicate dishes, and that complex full-bodied wines should accompany strong tasting meats, cheeses and powerful sauces.

Thus, a rich beef stew will generally overpower a light white wine, and a powerful red wine will generally be too much for a broiled fish fillet. Another useful rule of thumb is that if a wine was used to make a sauce or a casserole, you should drink the same wine used in the food.

The table at the end of this chapter outlines some suggestions that are generally accepted by the connoisseurs as correct. Nobody will be able to criticize your taste if you follow these rules.

Fortified wines should generally not be drunk with food. The sugar in the sweeter wines tends to depress the appetite, and the herbs and spices of the flavored wines competes with the flavor of the food. Thus, the dry sherries and the flavored wines, such as the vermouths, should be served before meals, and the sweet ports and sherries should be served afterwards.

## Serving Temperatures

As a general rule, the lighter and fresher the wine, the cooler should be the temperature at which it is served. White and rosé wines should be served chilled, because if the wine is too warm, the natural acidity is reduced, and the wine loses its character.

Full-bodied red wines should be served at a warmer temperature. The warmth seems to reduce the sharpness and to increase the aroma. You often hear that these wines should be served at room temperature, whereas we suggest that the wine should be served at about 70 degrees, cooler than most rooms. The words "room temperature" originated in England, where 65-70 degrees is, indeed, the temperature in most rooms!

The table at the end of the chapter shows the ideal temperature at which each type of wine should be served. You should try to serve it within about five degrees of the temperatures shown.

If the wine has not been stored at the temperature at which you will drink it, try to bring it gradually to the right temperature, since rushing the job seems to have quite an effect on the taste. It is best to bring a bottle of fine old Burgundy from its 55 degree storage space several hours before you intend to serve it rather than putting it into a bucket of hot water.

On the other hand, the practice of putting a white wine into an ice bucket for twenty minutes or so seems to do it no harm. An hour in the refrigerator does as well. It is, however, better to serve it slightly too warm than to put it in the freezer to accelerate the cooling.

Too many restaurants keep their white wine in a refrigerator, and serve it much too cold, at about 40 degrees. At this temperature, the aroma does not get a chance to escape, and much of the pleasure is lost. If this happens to you, ask to have the wine taken out of the ice bucket and let it warm up at the table. You can also warm the wine in your glass by holding it with the bowl in the palms of your hands.

## Glasses

At a really formal dinner, several different wines will usually be served, each one in a different type of glass. This is excessive for most people, and it is generally enough to have one, or at most two types of glasses to serve your wine.

If you are going to have two types of glasses, we recommend a large glass (eight ounces or more) for red wines, and a smaller glass (six to eight ounces) for white and rosé wines. If you are going to have only one type of glass, as most people do, you should stay with the larger eight ounce size.

There are only two factors that are important for wine glasses. The first is that the glass be clear and colorless, preferably without ornamentation. How can you possibly judge the color and clarity of a wine if the glass itself is colored?

The second factor is the shape of the glass. The glass should have a stem, so that you can hold it without warming the wine too much, and it should be wider at the top than at the bottom, so that the aroma can escape. Ideally, the top of the glass should be slightly narrower than the middle, but this is not critical.

The serving of Champagne, and other sparkling wines deserves a special mention. Historically, Champagne was served in flat, open glasses, which, in fact, are the worst possible shape! The pleasure of drinking Champagne comes from the aroma and from the sparkling fresh taste provided by the bubbles.

The aroma is lost from the flat glasses, and this shape also causes the bubbles to escape in a very few minutes. If you drink Champagne frequently, it is worth investing in special long, thin tulip shaped Champagne glasses. Otherwise you should use the normal six to eight ounce glasses used for white wine.

Even though the long tulip shaped glasses have been socially required for the last several years, many restaurants and professional caterers still supply only the old-fashioned flat glasses for parties and weddings. This is probably because they are less fragile, and are much easier to wash.

However, they are not acceptable for Champagne, and should only be used to serve ice cream, or other desserts. If you are going to spend a lot of money to serve Champagne, why use glasses that are socially incorrect and also ruin the wine?

## Opening the Wine

Opening a bottle of wine would not appear to be a very difficult task, but it can cause problems and even embarrassment at times. Very old bottles of wine present their own problems, as does the opening of Champagne, both of which we shall cover.

Inexpensive jug wines often come with a metal cap that you are supposed to twist, breaking off a ring at the bottom of the cap, which then comes off the bottle. Unfortunately, sometimes when you twist the cap, the ring doesn't break off, and you can't get the cap off the bottle! Alternatively, it is sometimes impossible to twist the cap at all.

If you look closely at the place where the ring (the one that was supposed to break off) joins the rest of the cap, you will see a number of points around the ring where it is attached to the cap. The force of twisting the cap is supposed to break these, separating the ring from the cap.

If these are not broken, saw at each of these points with a serrated knife (a steak knife does well) until they do break, at which point the cap should come off.

The key to opening a wine bottle that has been sealed with a cork (all fine wines) is to have a good corkscrew. Corkscrews come in many different shapes and sizes, but they all fit into one of three categories, one of which is good, one of which is adequate, and one of which, in our judgment, can be dangerous.

Some cork removers work on the principle of injecting a gas or air into the bottle until the pressure in the bottle becomes so great that the cork is forced out. This is unquestionably the easiest way of getting the cork out of the bottle, and there is virtually no chance of pushing the cork into the bottle.

However, if there is a fault in the bottle, there is some chance that it may explode before the cork comes out. This seems to be a rather dangerous way of saving some effort.

The two remaining types of corkscrew work on the principle of winding a metal thread into the cork. The thread stays in place in the cork while you pull the whole thing, cork and all, out of the bottle.

One type uses some leverage against the top of the bottle to get the cork out, while the other requires that you hold the bottle steady and pull very hard to get the cork out.

The corkscrew that uses leverage, rather than brute force, is not only considerably easier to use, but also ensures that the cork is removed with a steady pull, which reduces the chance of breaking it. There are many types on the market, and it does not make much difference which one you get.

When you are opening a bottle of wine, first remove the foil from around the top of the bottle. The top of the cork, thus exposed, sometimes looks rather unattractive, with some mould or dried wine. This is generally not serious, unless a great deal of wine has escaped, allowing air to enter the wine. You should, however, clean off the top of the bottle so that none of the dirt gets into the wine.

Next, measure the length of the cork against the corkscrew. The corkscrew should be twisted into the cork until the tip is just at the bottom of the cork, without actually going through the bottom.

If you misjudge the length, and go through the cork, it doesn't matter very much. The worst that will happen is that you will get a few small pieces of cork in the first glass that you pour (which should be yours!).

Using a steady, even pressure, you then pull the corkscrew out of the bottle, without twisting it. If you have a corkscrew that uses leverage, the action of the corkscrew against the top of the bottle will provide sufficient force to remove even the most tightly fitting cork without too much effort.

If you have one that does not use leverage, you may have a problem if the cork is stiff and does not come out easily. The bottle is likely to move rapidly when the cork finally does come out. We thus recommend that you always steady the bottle by holding it with the bottom on the table or on the floor (or even between your knees, which is not very elegant but is effective). This will avoid the embarrassment and waste of wine flying acrosss the room when you are opening a difficult bottle.

Sometimes the cork will break in the middle, particularly if the corkscrew was not far enough into the cork, and only half of the cork will come out. Then you have a problem. The neck of the bottle is narrower at the top of the cork than at the bottom, so, unless you are very careful (and lucky), you are likely to push the broken half into the bottle. The trick is to push down as little as possible while you twist the corkscrew into what is left of the cork.

If you are lucky, you will get a good purchase on the cork, and pull it out. If not, the cork will fall into the wine. If this happens, it will not do the wine any harm. It doesn't look very elegant, but it happens to everyone from time to time.

As you tip the bottle, the cork will float out of the way, and you can pour the wine out in the normal way. As an aside, if you are on a picnic, and forget the corkscrew, simply clean the top of the bottle, pierce the cork (so the air can escape) and push it into the bottle.

You need to be especially careful if you are fortunate enough to be opening a very old bottle of wine. The cork may be crumbling and very likely to break; also the wine will almost certainly contain a great deal of sediment, which must not be shaken up.

When you take an old bottle out of storage, take great care not to shake it or to turn it, since the sediment will all be on the side of the bottle that was at the bottom. The bottle should be laid in a basket, or some container that allows it to remain almost horizontal, with the neck slightly up. You should then remove the foil and clean the top of the bottle in the normal way.

If you have one of the corkscrews that inject air or gas into the bottle, this is the one time that you can use it to help you, so long as you do not try to use the pressure to push the cork out entirely. Gently insert the needle right through the cork, and inject a small amount of gas into the bottle so that there is some pressure pushing against the cork from the inside of the bottle. Old bottles are more likely to explode than new ones, so it is even more dangerous to use much pressure.

The procedure is now the same whether you have used the air pressure corkscrew or have not. It is essential to get the corkscrew in almost to the bottom of the cork, because an old cork is very likely to break if you don't. You then pull the cork out, slowly and carefully, in the normal way.

After opening any wine, always pour a little of the wine into your own glass first. It is polite to make sure that you, as the host, get any small pieces of cork that may have fallen into the wine. You pour the wine for everyone else at the table before filling your own glass. You should never fill a wine glass more than two thirds full or the aroma will be lost.

If you are suspicious of the wine, you may want to taste it before serving it to your guests, but you should generally do this away from the table. The wines where you are the most likely to have problems are the full-bodied red wines, and you should have ample opportunity to taste it when you open the wine some time prior to serving it.

Special considerations also apply when you are opening a bottle of Champagne, or another sparkling wine. For these wines, the difficulty is to avoid having the cork come out with so much force that it flies out of control and, worse, some of the wine is lost.

This can be avoided with a little care. The first thing to remember is to keep your hand over the top of the cork while opening the bottle. You should also chill sparkling wines before opening the bottle, since cooling the wine reduces the pressure considerably. It is also important to remember not to shake the bottle before you open it, since this tends to release the gas in the bottle, and increases the pressure.

As you look at the foil covering the top of the bottle, you will see the outline of the wire cage that holds the cork in the bottle. You will see a small ring in the wire, which has been made by twisting it tight at this point. This ring is usually lying flat against the bottle, and you should pull it up with your fingernail or a knife. This will tear the foil if you have not already removed it (which you do not need to do).

You now untwist the ring so that the whole wire cage becomes loose, and can be removed, taking the rest of the foil with it. You should have a glass ready by the bottle, because once the cork does come out, some wine almost always fizzes out immediately. If the cork does not come out on its own, you should tip the bottle about half way between vertical and horizontal, with the neck over the glass.

Holding the bottle in one hand and the cork in the other, you should now twist one while holding the other (the experts say that you should twist the bottle, while holding the cork steady, but we have never found that it makes much difference which one is twisted). Once the cork is loosened in the neck of the bottle, it should come out with a splendid pop without further effort on your part.

If you have to pull at the cork after it is loose in the bottle, or if there is no pop, the chances are that the gas has escaped, and the wine is flat. Flat Champagne is not worth drinking, and the bottle should be returned.

## Decanting Wines

Decanting is the process of pouring the wine from its original bottle into another container. Full-bodied red wines should always be decanted, as should sweet white wines that have thrown a sediment. Light red wines, dry white wines and sparkling wines should never be decanted.

The purpose of decanting mature wines is to separate the wine from the sediment, so that none of the sediment is poured into your glass.

After removing the cork, the bottle should be left on its side with the neck of the bottle slightly raised and the sediment on the side of the bottle towards the bottom. Raise the bottle slightly, and pour the wine slowly into a decanter (or any other clean container) until the first evidence of sediment appears in the neck of the bottle.

A source of light, often a candle, is usually placed on the

other side of the bottle to make the spotting of the sediment easier. As soon as the first signs of sediment appear, all the wine that is fit to drink will be in the decanter. The wine left in the bottle should be discarded with the sediment.

The purpose of decanting young full-bodied red wines (which rarely have any sediment to worry about) is to mix some air in with the wine as it is being decanted, so that the oxygen can soften the taste.

Over a short period of time, a few hours at most, oxygen helps to speed up the maturing process without turning the wine to vinegar. In addition, the aroma of a very young red wine is often rather weak when the bottle is first opened, and the air reacting with the wine causes this aroma to become stronger. When this happens, the wine is said to have "opened up," having been "closed in" while the aroma was weak.

If the wine is not decanted, it is advisable to open a bottle of young full-bodied red wine some time before it is to be drunk. This allows the wine to come in contact with the air at the top of the bottle. This process is called "allowing the wine to breathe".

A good rule of thumb is that you should let a full-bodied red wine breathe in the bottle for one hour for every year that the wine is less than ten years old. In other words, a Bordeaux that is four years old should breathe for about six hours.

Unfortunately, there is rarely enough time to let the wine breathe for the required period. If you do not have several hours to let it breathe, decanting it is a very good way of speeding up the process.

For young full-bodied red wines, you should be rather rough with the wine and pour it into the decanter in such a way as to create large air bubbles in the wine. It should then be allowed to sit for a good twenty minutes or so. The effect of decanting the wine this way will be roughly the same as if you had been able to let the wine breathe in the bottle for an additional three or four hours!

Even though there is a strong argument in favor of decanting all full-bodied red wines, very few restaurants are receptive when you ask for a young one to be decanted. Those restaurants selling old red wines at high prices generally know enough to decant them.

We suspect that the reason is that attractive decanters are expensive and are very tedious to wash after use. However, these wines are often quite expensive, and you should insist that any full-bodied red wine be decanted regardless of its age. If the restaurant does not have a decanter for your three-year-old Cabernet Sauvignon, a water jug will do just as well.

As consumers become more knowledgeable about the subject, it is probable that more restaurants will routinely offer to decant these wines. In the meantime, however, you will normally have to push for it to be done!

## Wine as Alcohol

Most wine contains between 8% and 12% alcohol, and is thus twice as strong as beer, and about one quarter as strong as whiskey or gin. However, a normal sized glass of wine is about six ounces; thus, a glass of wine contains the same amount of alcohol as a martini or a can of beer.

The misconception that wine is less harmful than other drinks seems to have two roots. The first is that it is a natural drink, and contains many useful vitamins and minerals. There is even an increasing body of evidence that wine, in moderation, is actually good for you. The same is not true for excessive amounts, however.

The second argument heard is that one does not get drunk on wine as rapidly as one does when drinking other things. This is, indeed, often true, but the reason is that wine is usually accompanied by food, and there is clear evidence that food in the stomach slows down the absorption of alcohol.

Slowing down the absorption is not the same as reducing it, and it still ends up in the bloodstream. It takes just as long for the body to eliminate the alcohol from wine as it does to eliminate it from any other drink.

## Serving Wine

| Wine | Temperature (Degrees F.) | Correct Food |
|---|---|---|
| *Table Wines* | | |
| Full-Bodied Red | 70 | Red meat, casseroles, rich sauces, strong cheeses. |
| Light Red | 60 | Most meat, poultry, light sauces, pasta. |
| Dry White | 50 | Best wine for fish, but can be drunk with any dish. |
| Sweet White | 50 | Desserts, fruit, nuts. |
| Rosé | 50 | Any dish. |
| Sparkling | 45 | Best with dessert, but can be drunk with any dish. |
| *Fortified Wines* | | |
| Dry or Flavored | 50 | Before meals. |
| Sweet | 70 | After meals or sometimes with dessert. |

# 4. How to Buy Wine

The purpose of this chapter is to give you guidance about buying wine in a store, in a restaurant or for a wedding or a large party. It also covers the wine labeling laws of the United States, so that you know what information must be on the label of any wine sold in this country.

*Buying Wine*

With the increasing awareness of the do's and don'ts of wine, most sellers of wine are storing and selling their wines in a responsible fashion. However, there are still many that do not, and who routinely sell poor or spoiled wines at inflated prices. They can usually get away with this, because they know that most people will accept a relatively small loss in order to avoid an unpleasant confrontation.

The following comments primarily apply if you are thinking about buying a relatively expensive wine, particularly a full-bodied red wine. Most other wines should be drunk young, and are less likely to have been spoiled by poor storage conditions.

As you go into a wine store or restaurant, there are a number of clues to watch out for. If you spot these clues, it does not necessarily mean that you should not buy any wine in that store, merely that you should decide on a different wine. Instead of a good, expensive Burgundy, buy a young light red wine, a Beaujolais or an Italian Bardolino. These are much less likely to disappoint you.

Most establishments know enough to store wine on its side, so that the cork does not dry out, but we have seen stores with the wine standing up on the shelves. If this is the case, you should avoid any wine more than a year or so old.

Do not buy any good wine that may have been on display in the shop window, particularly if it has been subjected to direct sunlight. Not only will the wine have suffered from too much light, but also the sun will have heated the wine during the day, and the temperature will have dropped at night. This will destroy any wine in a very short time.

The better establishments will store most of their stock in temperature-controlled wine cellars. Only the wines expected to be sold within a very short period will be out of the cellar. You should always ask how the wine has been stored before buying any expensive wine.

If you learn that the stock is stored in the main area of the wine store, or restaurant, you should, again, only buy the young wines. We have seen very old Bordeaux wines, from some of the best estates, sit for months in a corner of a wine store. These wines, priced at over one hundred dollars a bottle eventually disappeared.

Clearly, the wine must have been ruined, and the buyer of the wine should have returned it to the store for a full refund. After reading this book, we hope that you will have the confidence to return a bad bottle if you happen to get one. However, it is always better to avoid a problem before it happens!

In the chapters on the wines from various countries, we give you some suggestions on how to select the wines from each country. There are some specific guidelines that should be used, regardless of the country of origin.

You should generally buy wines that have specific quality classifications and which are made from defined grape varietals. Although these will be priced at premium over cheaper blended wines, this premium need not be too great if you know what you are doing.

Chapter 7 discusses the value that you should place on official classifications, and how to use them. They generally assure you that the wine has been made according to the regulations, and give you some indication of what the wine should be like. This is not true for the unclassified wines, where the name of the wine may actually be misleading.

With some exceptions, you should stay away from wines backed by massive publicity campaigns. This is particularly true for wines widely promoted on television, where advertising time is extremely expensive.

Good wine is not a mass production product, and any wine that is made in sufficient quantities to justify a massive advertising campaign is unlikely to be particularly good. In addition, the profits from the wine have to be very large to cover the advertising costs, so there is not too much money left over to cover the costs of making the wine.

We have one final suggestion that can save you some embarrassment. When you give an important dinner party, for your boss, for example, the last thing that you want is for the wine to be bad. If you are buying the wine especially for the dinner party, you should always buy it two or three days before the dinner and try a bottle before the big day.

If the wine is good, you will have had a bonus of a nice bottle of wine. In addition, you will have had a chance to evaluate it, without being under any social pressure. You will then be better able to talk about it if the guest is a connoisseur.

This suggestion is more important if the wine is bad. You will know this before the big day, and will have the time to take it back and exchange it for a better wine, which you should also try.

So long as you don't drink much of the wine from the

bad bottle, the wine store should give you a refund for all of the wine, including the bottle that you opened. Nobody, but you, will know how close you came to disaster!

## Investing in Wine

Wine is sometimes bought as an investment. This is generally a very poor idea, unless the "return" on your investment is going to be the pleasure of drinking it when it is mature. It is illegal, in most states, to sell wine without a license. Thus, it is difficult to get your money out, even when you see similar wines going for several times what you paid.

There are a few auctions for fine wines. The only wines that get good prices are full cases of the very top names, from well-known private collections, or from the cellars of the specialty wine houses. Before buyers will pay top prices, they have to know the history of the wines and be sure that they have been stored under perfect conditions.

We often see pathetic letters to the wine magazines, asking about the value of a bottle of old wine that has been kept for several years. The writers must surely be very disappointed to learn that the wines are essentially worthless. Frequently, they are also way over the hill by the time the letter was written and are not even fit to drink! After reading this book, this should not happen to you.

If you have good storage conditions, by all means, buy fine wines to drink over the years. However, do not buy them in the hope of making a profit. This should be left to the professionals.

## Wine for Weddings and Parties

Special considerations apply if you are buying wine for a

special occasion, such as a wedding or a big party, especially if you are using a professional caterer.

It is the responsibility of the caterer to serve the wine at the correct temperature, and you should accept no excuses for this not being done. Warm Champagne is just as unpleasant at a large party as it is at home and will cause you embarrassment as well. Furthermore, you should select the wines that go well with the food you intend to serve, as described in Chapter 3.

In the Wine Appreciation Course (chapter 6) we suggest that the best way to learn about wine is to compare several wines of the same general type. Even if you do not follow this course, it is especially useful to have a one-shot comparative tasting before an important occasion. Too many people forget that their interests and those of the caterer do not necessarily coincide, and they accept the advice of the caterer without thinking.

As a result, they often end up buying the wine with the highest markup for the caterer, rather than the best value for the money. This is particularly true for Champagne, where the difference between the prices of two Champagnes of similar quality can amount to several dollars per bottle.

Once you have decided on the type of wine to be served, you should buy several different wines of that type, and taste them side by side. If you are not yet comfortable with your judgment, you can invite someone whose judgment you trust to taste the wines with you, and discuss each wine as you taste it.

As you do this, you will find yourself becoming more expert by the minute, and you will be in a much better position to make the trade-offs between price and quality. You will often find that you can choose a less expensive wine that you like as much as the more expensive ones.

There is usually a high markup on wine, and prices are often more negotiable than you might think. A few minutes of hard bargaining will frequently result in significant savings.

Moreover, you should always demand to pay for only the wine (or hard liquor) actually consumed, with the right to return all unopened bottles for a refund.

It is absolutely essential that you, personally, check the inventory before the party begins, and again immediately it is over. You should make certain that the empty bottles plus the full bottles equal the number of bottles that you started with. This way, you will not get charged for bottles that "disappear".

Sometimes the caterer will quote a price that includes "all the wine you can drink". Unless you know that your guests are particularly hard drinkers, this is generally a bad deal for you. The caterer will make a high estimate of how much will be drunk, and will then add on an additional amount to cover his risk. Furthermore, he will probably instruct the bartender to serve the drinks as slowly as possible.

You will thus end up paying more money for less wine than your guests really want, possibly spoiling the party as well. If you want to keep the costs down, it is much better for you to be the one to tell the bartender to slow down, once the party is in full swing.

## *Ordering Wine in a Restaurant*

There are some special issues that come up when you are buying wine in a restaurant. For many people, the approach of the wine waiter, with his impressive and often confusing wine list, is a threatening experience.

By now, you should be in a better position to cope with the situation. In Chapter 5 we discuss the procedure you should adopt when evaluating any wine. You should carry out these same procedures in a restaurant, preferably with a relaxed and confident manner. In this way, you will impress the wine waiter with your expertise, and will take control of the situation.

There are also some steps you should take before even ordering the wine, in order to give yourself the best possible chance. This may involve changing the way you normally go about ordering the meal, but we believe that this small change is important.

When Americans go into a restaurant, they usually sit down, have a round or two of cocktails, order the meal, and only then order the wine. Since cocktails are usually the most profitable item served at the restaurant, this clearly suits the restaurant owners. However, it is often not in your best interests.

The key to enjoying your wine in a restaurant is to follow the procedures that the French use. You should order the wine as soon as you possibly can. This will give a full-bodied red wine more time to breathe, and will give white and rosé wines enough time to reach the right temperature, without being hurried.

You should ask for the menu and the wine list immediately upon sitting down. Once the food decisions have been made, you are ready to select the wine(s). If everyone is having similar dishes, the same wine will suit everybody. The problem arises when some people are having fish, while others are having steak.

All too often, a rosé wine is ordered as a compromise. The thought is that since the wine is slightly red, it will go with the meat, and since it is not very red, it will not overpower the fish. Of course, since few rosé wines have any distinction, the result is that nobody is truly satisfied.

In fact, there are two better solutions. The first is to ask each person for his or her preference. There are some people that prefer one type of wine, regardless of the food which it is to accompany. If this solution provides unanimous agreement, your problem is solved!

If you do not get total agreement, you still have another

avenue to explore. If there are more than three or four people at the table, you will probably need more than one bottle. It is perfectly correct to order two different wines at the same time, so that everybody is satisfied.

Sometimes, however, two full bottles is too much, or the demand is not evenly divided. Since most appetizers go well with white wine, you may be able to solve your problem by ordering a full bottle of white wine with the appetizers, and a half bottle of red wine to follow.

In this case, you take care not to drink all of the white wine with the appetizers. This wine will continue to be drunk by those who ordered the fish, while those eating the steaks will have the red wine with the main dish, and again you will have satisfied everybody. We leave to your own creativity the other solutions you can come up with using combinations of wines, and the use of half bottles.

An expert does not mispronounce the names of the wines he is ordering. The sommelier will know that the client knows little about wine if he pronounces Graves (a district of Bordeaux) as "Grayves" as opposed to the correct "Grahve".

German and Italian wines are pronounced exactly as written, except that, in Italian, you should generally stress the syllable before the last one.

French wines are more difficult to pronounce, but should be pronounced roughly correctly. A perfect accent is not necessary, but one should not, for example, pronounce letters that are silent in French (such as the final 's' in Graves). You will find an English approximation of the pronunciation of the major French wines when they appear in the index at the end of this book (in parentheses after the name of the wine).

We have covered the issue of the failure to store wine properly, but many restaurants still expect you to pick up the tab for this. If you ever get a bad bottle of wine, you should never hesitate to send it back and refuse to pay for it.

Once you have sent back a wine, we strongly recommend

that you then order a different one. Sometimes, you will have had bad luck with a single bottle, which may not have been properly cleaned when the wine was bottled, and other bottles of the same wine will be good.

Our experience, however, has taught us that when one bottle is bad, all of the other bottles of the same batch are usually also bad. This is usually the result of poor storage somewhere along the line between the vineyard and the table. Thus, if we return a full-bodied red wine, we usually switch to a young light red wine, or even a white wine.

The decor of many restaurants often includes attractive looking racks of wines on the wall. Unfortunately, the temperature in the restaurant is likely to be around 75 degrees when it is open for business, and the heating (or cooling) will be turned off when the restaurant is closed.

Needless to say, these temperature variations are bad for the wine, and you should only buy very young wines in such a restaurant, unless most of the stock is stored in a proper wine cellar.

There are unfortunately, some other practices in restaurants that you should watch out for. Wine lists are expensive to produce, and many restaurants are rather imprecise in describing their wines. In this way, when they run out of a particular wine, they can replace it with one that is roughly the same, without having to reprint the wine list. While we sympathize, it is very difficult to select a good wine when the description is incomplete!

For example, you will often see a wine described as "Médoc, Vintage". This does tell you that the wine was almost certainly made from the Cabernet Sauvignon grape varietal, and that the wine was made in the Médoc district of Bordeaux, in France.

However, you don't know whether it is a highly rated Estate Bottled wine, or a relatively inexpensive blend from many estates; nor do you know which vintage it is, who made it or who imported it. In other words, you simply do not have enough information to make an intelligent decision.

Furthermore, it is not unusual for a restaurant to have two different wines, both of which are legally entitled to be called "Médoc". The quality of the two wines will be very different, even though they are to be sold at the same price. The better one is only served to those customers who know enough to ask intelligent questions.

If you do not have enough information, it is both correct and advisable for you to ask the wine waiter for more information. In addition, once you have limited your choice to two or three possible wines, it is perfectly proper for you to request that the bottles be brought for your inspection and final decision.

In Bordeaux, for example, there are hundreds of estates, and it is impossible to remember them all. The wine waiter knows this, and it is one of the signs of an expert that you not be afraid to ask for advice when you come across a wine list with few, if any, names that you recognize.

His job is to know his stock and to know which wines are good (value), and which are less so. Your job is to look good, and to ask the right questions in such a way that he gives you good advice and does not trade on your ignorance to unload an inferior wine on you.

While outright fraud is somewhat rare, it does happen from time to time. One thing that we have often seen is that the vintage on the bottle is different from that on the wine list. The usual explanation is that the restaurant sold all of an earlier vintage and replaced the wine with one of a more recent year. Whatever the reason, you may want to reconsider your decision.

You should never accept a wine that has not been presented to you, unopened, for your inspection. Furthermore, the wine should be opened right at your table. The reason is to make sure that the wine you get is the wine you ordered and are paying for.

Dishonest restaurants often gamble on the ignorance of the customer. If the wine is opened in the back, out of your sight, there is a possibility of some of the good wine you are paying for being poured out of the bottle and replaced with water or an inferior wine. Since all restaurants know that the wine should be opened at the table, any attempt to open the wine elsewhere should make you highly suspicious.

## *Wine Labeling Laws in the United States*

Certain information must be shown on the labels of all wines distributed or produced in the United States. In addition, there are certain quality related optional terms that the winemaker may wish to use. If these optional items appear on the label, the information must be true. The mandatory and optional requirements and the meaning of each item are listed at the end of this chapter.

For most of the requirements, the information will be in English, although the foreign language is also permitted for some of the quality indicators. In the chapters on wines from other countries, we provide both the English and the foreign language versions.

We are not attorneys, and this list is not precise enough to use if you intend to make or sell wine. However, it is our understanding of the present law in enough detail to be useful.

In addition to those terms covered by law, the producer may use other marketing words, such as "fine," "reserved," "superior," and so on, provided that he does not use any of the reserved terms in the table. These phrases, which usually appear on the back label are essentially meaningless!

Furthermore, wines imported from countries which have stringent wine labeling laws, have the same protection in the United States that they have in their own country.

Thus, if you are drinking a French wine, that uses terms that are defined under French law (e.g. *Appellation Contrôlée*) you know that the wine will conform to the French requirements for this description.

You do, however, have to make sure that the wine was made in the country from which a famous name originates. Many wines made in the United States, or in other countries, such as Spain, use generic names such as Burgundy, Chablis, Rhine and Chianti that are protected under the laws of the European country where the wine was originally from.

If the wine was not made in the country from which the name originates, there is no protection whatsoever. Many of the large mass merchandising corporations make enormous quantities of jug wines, often calling them "Chablis," "Burgundy," or some other respected name.

These are usually light wines, ready for immediate consumption. They are generally inferior blends of undistinguished grape varietals, and are often as expensive as other, and better, wines. Apart from the color, they seldom bear any resemblance to the European wines whose names they carry, and the quality is invariably much lower.

There is even a rumor that at least one winemaker sells a wine under the label "California Chablis" and another labeled "California Rhine," both of which come out of the same batch of wine!

Although this practice is permitted by law, we find it confusing, and a disservice to the consumer. You are likely to be turned off all Burgundies if you meet one of these wines, and are not warned that the California "Burgundy" on the table is in a completely different league from the real thing.

Many U.S. winemakers do, indeed, make wines that are comparable to these European wines in taste and in quality. However, these wines will invariably use the more prestigious varietal label, rather than the generic term. For example, if a producer is going to make a wine that is like a Chablis, he will use the Chardonnay grape varietal, and sell the wine as a Chardonnay, at a higher price.

## Label Information

| *Information* | *Requirements* |
|---|---|
| *Mandatory (all wines)* | |
| Country of origin | The wine must come from that country |
| Producer | The name and location of the firm that made and bottled the wine. |
| Importer (for imported wines) | The name and location, in the U. S. of the firm that imported the wine and is responsible that it comply with U. S. laws. |
| Alcoholic Content | The percentage of pure alcohol in the wine. |
| Net Contents | The volume of the wine in the bottle. |
| "Wine" | If the word "wine" is used without the addition an another fruit (e.g. peach), it means that the liquid was made entirely from grapes. |

Optional information and requirements follow on the next page.

## Label Information (continued)

| Information | Requirements |
|---|---|
| *Optional (superior wines)* | |
| Official Classification (imported) | The local country regulations for the classification of origin and/or quality must have been met. |
| Region | If a region is mentioned, and the region is in the country where the wine was made, the wine must come from that region. |
| Grape Varietal | For a varietal to be on the label, at least 75% by volume (51% before 1980) must come from the varietal named. |
| Vintage | If a vintage year is shown, all of the wine must have come from grapes harvested in the year shown. |
| Estate Bottled | If the label represents that the wine is Estate Bottled, then the grapes must have been grown, and the wine made and bottled on the estate. |

# 5. What to Look for in Wine

The purpose of this chapter is to provide you with a guide to evaluating any wine that you may come across. We also recommend the procedures that you should follow when tasting a wine so that you can show those around you that you know exactly what you are doing. Thus, your word will carry much more weight if you need to complain about the wine.

By following the systematic approach that we describe, you will be able to identify and evaluate the few factors that are important. In the process, you will not only become much more confident of your taste in selecting wines for your own table, but will also become more comfortable in discussing any wine with the experts.

## *Procedure*

At first you may feel a little self-conscious about following the procedures that we recommend, particularly while you are still at the learning stage. However, we do urge that you follow them carefully, for two reasons.

The first is to make sure that you do systematically evaluate all of the factors that are important in deciding on the quality of the wine. The second, particularly when you are being served wine in a restaurant, is that by using the same procedures that the true connoisseurs employ, you will establish yourself as an expert, whether you are or not.

In order to get the most information possible from a wine you need to use as many of your senses as you can. You need to look at the wine, to smell it, to taste it and to get the feel of it on your tongue. You can sometimes even use your fifth sense, by listening to the comments of the people around you!

The first step is to look at the cork from the bottle. If you are drinking an old wine, it is possible that the cork has deteriorated to the point that air has entered the bottle, and the wine will be undrinkable. This is very rare, but it can happen. The way to detect it is to sniff at the cork, and see whether it smells mouldy. If it does, the wine is said to be "corked," and the wine will be bitter and may also taste of vinegar.

A second reason for looking at the cork is to make sure that the wine inside the bottle is the same as that shown on the label. Fine wines are becoming so expensive, that there are dishonest merchants and importers around who will float the label off an empty bottle of expensive wine and attach it to a bottle of inferior wine.

It is much more difficult to remove and replace a cork, and most producers of good wines brand their corks with the name of the estate and often the vintage as well. The less prosperous estates have less detail on the cork, but there is usually enough information to give you a good indication of the wine in the bottle. If the name is not there, you have reason to be suspicious of the wine, and should evaluate it very carefully.

Once you have satisfied yourself about the cork, you should turn your attention to the wine itself. Make sure that you have at least three tablespoons of wine in your glass. If you get only a teaspoonful or so, do not hesitate about asking for more, since it is difficult to evaluate a wine if you do not have enough.

Pick up the glass and hold it between you and a source of

light. This will allow you to judge the color and appearance of the wine. Although neither is critical in your enjoyment, both will give you some important clues about its quality. These clues are discussed in the next section of this chapter.

The next step is to pick up the glass and swirl the wine around so that most of the inside of the glass is moistened. This effectively increases the surface area of the wine and releases the aroma of the wine into the top of the glass.

Next comes the easiest, and certainly the most important step in the whole process. You stick your nose inside the glass and take a deep sniff! Each grape varietal has its own characteristic aroma, and this one sniff will tell you whether the wine is as labeled, and it will give you important clues about the overall quality of the wine.

While the sense of smell is very important for a good wine, it is even more important to give you a warning that the wine may actually be bad. When the wine smells of vinegar, or if it has almost no aroma at all, it is likely that you have a problem!

Once you have judged the appearance and the aroma of the wine, the time has come to taste it. This is not quite as simple as it sounds since the tongue can only differentiate between sweet, sour, bitter and salty. Although the first three may be present in a wine, there are other qualities that are more important!

You need to mix some air in with the wine in your mouth, and to use your full sense of smell as well as that of taste to get a good idea of what it is like.

The way to do this is to take a reasonably large sip of wine and to suck a little air in through the wine before swallowing any. You need to be careful not to choke on the wine, and it may be a good idea to practise this with some water in the bathroom before trying it in public with wine!

This step will not only give you an overall sense of the wine, but will also verify your earlier suspicions that the wine may have turned to vinegar, or be over the hill (if there was no aroma) or that the deterioration of the cork may have spoiled it.

Another factor to consider is the degree of sharpness and acidity that you taste. All wine should have some acidity, otherwise it would taste dull and insipid. However, a wine that tastes too sour should be downgraded, particularly if you are drinking a white wine, a rosé or a light red wine. All of these are intended to be drunk young, and they should have only enough acidity to make the wine refreshing.

If a wine tastes bitter, the bottle is almost certainly bad and should be returned. However, it can sometimes be difficult to determine whether a relatively young full-bodied red wine is bitter because it is bad or is merely very sharp because it is young. Obviously, it is not fair to return a wine that has not gone bad, but neither should you be expected to pay for one that has turned!

You have some allies to help you with this decision. The first is your sense of smell; the second is the air as time passes. Take another deep sniff at the wine. If the aroma of the grape varietal is strong and clear, the wine is almost certainly good and should probably not be returned. If not, it is more probable that you have a problem.

If you are still not sure, you should follow the normal procedure for full-bodied red wines, and decant it in the usual way. Then pour some more wine into your glass, and wait for as long as you possibly can before deciding. Explain to the wine waiter, if you are in a restaurant, that you are not sure about the wine, and that you wish to let it "breathe" for a while before accepting it. After fifteen or twenty minutes, taste it again.

If the wine is bad, it will taste even more bitter, and should be returned without further ado! On the other hand, if it is not actually bad, but just too young, it should have softened somewhat and have improved noticeably.

Once you have swallowed the sip, the last step is for you to concentrate on the finish, the aftertaste left in your mouth. If the wine has a rather weak finish, it is often possible to increase the effect by opening the mouth slightly and inhaling rapidly. This concentrates the flavors and makes them more apparent.

The first sip of the wine is by far the most important. Because the finish remains in the mouth, your evaluation of the aroma and taste of the second sip is strongly influenced by the first. This becomes even more significant if you are tasting two or more wines.

These are the steps that you should go through to evaluate any wine, and you should carry them out every time you drink wine. This way, each wine that you try will be added to your memory, and you will find it easier and easier to evaluate future wines.

## Evaluation

The first section of this chapter described the procedure to follow in judging a wine, and discussed in general terms the things to look for. This section defines in more detail the specific factors that go into the evaluation of the quality of the wine you are drinking.

One of the difficulties that all wine drinkers experience is that of describing differences between the aromas and tastes of different wines. Two people, for example, sniffing at the same wine, will often use different words for what they sense. One may say that the wine has a scent of raspberries, while the other may feel that the scent of the wine reminds him of honey. Since neither raspberries nor honey is permitted in the production of wine, a chemical analysis will not show the presence of either!

This makes life very confusing, until it is understood that even the experts agree that the actual words used to describe a wine are not important. There are no absolute rules as to what makes a pleasant wine. Each person is free to enjoy one wine rather than another, and to use whatever terms he feels appropriate.

There are some general criteria that are usually used when evaluating wines, and we recommend that you start with these. As with so many things in life, you will very rarely find a wine that scores perfectly on every one of these criteria. It is necessary to find a way of balancing them, so that you can compare two wines giving the right weighting to those factors that you, personally, find important.

Our suggestion is to use a numeric scale and to give each wine that you taste a grade showing how it scores on each criterion. When you add up the total score, you will know how the wine compares to others you have tasted.

Most people today use a 20 point scale to judge wines and then give the most weight to the factors that they feel to be important. Listed below are the most commonly accepted quality factors and the weightings that we, personally, use to evaluate wines. Please feel free to modify them to suit your own personal tastes.

You should be aware that the most commonly used scoring systems do not give an official weighting to the importance of the finish. We don't agree; we feel that the finish is among the most important factors and give it a significant score.

A wine that scores 17-20 is a wine that we find outstanding; 14-16 will be a wine that is well above average, and 11-13 is a wine that is perfectly drinkable, but not memorable. Any wine that scores below 10 is one that we will avoid in the future.

| | |
|---|---|
| Appearance | 1 |
| Color | 1 |
| Aroma | 4 |
| Vinegar | 1 |
| Sweetness | 2 |
| Acidity | 2 |
| Astringency/Bitter | 2 |
| Body | 1 |
| Flavor | 1 |
| Finish | 3 |
| General Quality | 2 |

The next section of this chapter tells you what to look for under each of these criteria. Obviously you will be looking for different things for different types of wine. For example, the correct taste for full-bodied red wines will be different from that of light red wines.

Where these differences are significant between wine types, each one will be discussed. Where differences are not highlighted, you may assume that the quality factors are the same for all wines.

*Appearance* With today's advanced techniques for wine making, it is inexcusable for a winemaker to produce a wine that is not absolutely clear, with no visible particles in the wine. Thus a brilliantly clear wine scores 1, and a wine that is almost clear scores zero. If the wine is distinctly cloudy, it is probably a bad bottle; in that case, it should also score zero, and will almost certainly score badly on other criteria.

Alternatively, it may be an old full-bodied wine (or a late-picked sweet white wine) whose natural sediment has been shaken up. There may be nothing wrong with the wine, which may, in fact, be superlative, but shaking it may have ruined it.

Sometimes, particularly for the fine old late-picked sweet

French Sauternes or German Rieslings, the sediment will be heavy, and all that is necessary is to stand up the bottle for 15-20 minutes and decant the wine when the sediment has settled to the bottom.

However, the sediment for most old full-bodied red wines is too light to settle in less than several hours, by which time the wine will have been ruined by the exposure to the air. If you are in a restaurant, it is reasonable to expect the owner to accept responsibility for the improper serving of the wine, and you should send it back. If you are at home, it is probably your fault that the wine has been shaken up, and you will have made an expensive mistake!

*Color* Although the color is not important in your enjoyment of the wine itself, it can give you some important clues about how the wine will taste. Each grape varietal and each winemaking method has an effect on the color (and on the taste) of the wine.

The correct color for each wine that we discuss in this book is given under the discussion of that wine, and you should look at the color to see if the color is correct.

For example, most full-bodied red wines should be a deep red. If you get a wine that is supposed to be a rich, full-bodied wine, and the color is rather pale, the wine will taste much lighter than it should.

Most wines, both red and white, take on a brownish color as they age. If this is very pronounced, the wine is likely to be too old. The color of a full-bodied red wine can also be used to tell you how mature it is. The more mature red Bordeaux wines, for example, are a dark red brick color, with some evidence of brown to show the age.

The color of a white wine can also give you some indications as to its quality. The rich wines from the Chardonnay and Riesling grape varietals should generally be a light golden yellow; if wines from these grapes are very pale, or have a slightly greenish tinge, it is an indication that the grapes may not have been totally ripe at the harvest, and it is probable that the wine will be somewhat too thin and also probably too acidic to be as good as it might be.

Thus, if the wine is the right color you should give it a score of one. Otherwise, give it a score of zero.

*Aroma* The experts divide the fragrance of wine into two categories, the "aroma," which refers to the scent given to the wine by the grape varietal(s) from which it was made, and the "bouquet," which refers to the subtle change in the scent of the wine as it ages in the bottle. We find this distinction to be rather artificial, and use "aroma" for both.

When you put your nose in the glass to test the aroma, you should get a clean, fresh scent which clearly demonstrates the fragrance of the grape varietal. As you become more experienced, one good sniff will usually tell you at once almost all that you need to know about the wine.

It will tell you that the wine was made from the correct grape varietal, that there is no trace of vinegar, and that the wine is not too badly over the hill. A wine that has this good, clean, fresh aroma will also probably taste good, and should also have a good finish. A wine whose aroma is not clear (the term "muddy" is often used) is also likely to be undistinguished in its taste and finish.

The absence of any aroma at all should also give you cause to suspect that the wine, particularly a full-bodied red wine, may be over the hill, and too old to drink.

Since aroma is so important, we have given it four points in the weighting. You should give it four for a perfect aroma (very rare), three if the aroma is very good, two for a pleasant fragrance, one if it is all right but is nothing special and zero for no aroma or a very muddy one.

*Vinegar* If the wine tastes of vinegar, air has spoiled the wine. Give the wine a score of zero, and do not drink it. Other bottles of the same wine will not necessarily have also spoiled, and you may wish to try another bottle. If there is no vinegary taste, give it a score of one.

*Sweetness*   Almost all good table wines should be absolutely dry, with no discernible sugar. As we have mentioned, the exceptions are the Sauternes wines from France and the late-picked Riesling wines from Germany.

Thus, a wine that is absolutely dry should score two, one with a very slightly sweet taste gets one, and a wine that is noticeably sweet gets zero. Some sparkling wines, notably Asti Spumanti and some Champagnes are made with a high sugar content. You should give them a good score if the degree of sweetness is what you expect.

*Acidity*   All wine is slightly acid, which is necessary to make it refreshing. However, the degree of acidity should be appropriate to the type of wine. In general, the wine should be sufficiently sharp to make it interesting, without being so sharp that it puckers up the inside of your mouth. White wines are generally somewhat acid, since they do not have the tannins provided by the skins of the red wines to give them character.

Thus a wine that is just acid enough to give the wine a little bite should score two, one that is somewhat too acidic or too flat should score one, and one that is very sour or has no bite at all should score zero.

*Astringency/Bitterness*   All wines generally have a touch of astringency (sharpness), which comes from the natural ingredients in the grapes. This is usually rather pronounced in full-bodied red wines, particularly when they are still young. This sharpness comes from the tannins and is absolutely necessary to give these wines their character.

At the same time, it is totally inappropriate for any wine

which is intended to be drunk young to have a markedly sharp taste.

Thus the scoring for the bitterness or sharpness of the wine should depend on the amount of this factor expected in the wine. A wine that has the right degree of astringency should be given a score of two; one with somewhat too much or too little, a score of one; and a wine that totally lacks character, or is very sharp or is bitter, should be given a score of zero.

The wine literature maintains that nobody has become ill through drinking bad wine, and this may be true, but we see no reason to take chances, and if a wine is truly bad, we feel that it should be discarded.

*Body* The body of a wine is an important quality factor, but is also one that is very difficult to describe in words. It is the sense of fullness or of weight that the wine gives in the mouth. It is also related to the complexity of the taste of the wine and the level of alcohol present.

Perhaps giving you some examples is the best way to explain it. A heavy espresso coffee would be full-bodied when compared to instant coffee made without enough coffee in the spoon. Coca-cola is full-bodied when compared to diet ginger ale. Whiskey is full-bodied when compared to vodka.

If the wine has the correct body for its type, you should give it a score of one. If the wine is too thin and does not have enough body, you should give it a zero. It is unusual for the wine to be too full-bodied.

*Flavor* The overall flavor of the wine is also difficult to describe but is also important. Not only should the wine have the correct taste for its type, but there should also be a balance between the acidity, sweetness, astringency and body of the wine. This balance is important, since it can improve or detract from your enjoyment.

For example, if a wine is too sweet, but is also very acid, it would score badly on each of these criteria. However, the acidity can cut the cloying sweetness of the wine and make it considerably more attractive.

Thus, you should judge the overall impression of the flavor and the balance between its various elements. A wine whose balance and overall flavor are excellent should score one. If these factors are totally out of balance, or if you simply do not like the taste of the wine, you should give it a score of zero.

*Finish*   The finish affects the taste of whatever follows, whether this be another sip of the same wine, a different wine or the food that the wine is accompanying. This is why there is so much talk of the right wine to accompany your meal.

Since it has such a powerful effect, we feel that the finish should have a significant weighting in your evaluation. We have thus given it a possible score of three.

If the wine leaves a very pleasant and fresh aftertaste in your mouth, you should give the wine a score of three. If the finish is pleasant, but not outstanding, give it a two. If it is neutral, neither particularly pleasant nor unpleasant, it deserves a one, and a disagreeable or bitter finish should get zero.

*General Quality*   Now that you have evaluated all of the individual characteristics of the wine, you need to spend a few seconds thinking about your overall impression of how the wine looked, smelled and tasted. In sum, you are asking the single question of how much you liked the wine.

If you liked it very much, give it a two. If you liked it somewhat, but it was nothing special, give it a one. If you did not like it, give it a zero!

Once you have scored the wine on each of the quality

(and personal taste) factors, add up the score, and you will have a good estimate of how well the wine suits your tastes.

If you feel that there are too many things to try to remember, we do have a short cut, which will help you to get most of the benefit with less effort. Again, we suggest a twenty point score, but there are only four factors to consider, each one of which scores five points:

How pleasant is the aroma?
How pleasant is the taste?
How pleasant is the finish?
Is the wine a good value for the money?

# 6. A Step by Step Approach to Wine Appreciation

The purpose of this chapter is to give you some practical guidance on how you can become as expert as you wish to become. The enjoyment of wine is very personal, and can only be based on practical experience. Unfortunately, all too often, experience consists of making the same mistakes over and over again.

We have used our experience to design a systematic program that makes sure that you will take few steps in the wrong direction. This program need not be expensive, and you can start at the beginning, or anywhere in the middle, depending on your present level of expertise. There is plenty of room for you to use your own discretion and follow your own taste.

We have taken the approach used by the wine professionals and modified it for those who only need to learn enough to enjoy wine. This method consists of three major activities, which may be carried out simultaneously or in sequence, and are as follows:

1. Look, listen and learn.
2. Try, taste and test.
3. Relish, remember and write.

## Look, Listen and Learn

The first step is easy (and free!). Just go into a liquor store with a wide selection of wines, look around and ask questions. There are a number of things to look for on a wine label, but it is difficult to remember them all just from reading this, or any other book. You will find it easier to fix them in your mind by looking at how the actual labels present the information.

As you look at a bottle from a particular country, try to remember the items that should be on the label, and what they mean. If, for example, it is a French wine, is it an *Appellation Contrôlée* wine?

Does it come from a major region (e.g. Bordeaux), a district (e.g. Haut-Médoc), or a commune (e.g. Pauillac)? Is it Estate (Château) bottled? Is the Château a Classified Growth? What vintage is it? All of these terms are defined and described in the chapter on wines from Bordeaux.

Once you have gleaned all the information you can from one label, take a look at a label from another but similar wine from the same region. Look for the similarities as well as the differences between the two wines.

You should always find out the reasons for any wide differences in the prices of two wines. If the prices of two similar wines are very different, you should look at the labels for the factors that are important in determining the quality of the wine.

Some types of wine are invariably more expensive than others, either because they are more expensive to make, such as Champagne, or because only a limited supply is made, and there is a lot of demand.

The Burgundy region of France, for example, produces relatively little wine, which is also very popular; thus French Burgundy tends to be expensive. Even one that is merely entitled to the *Appellation Bourgogne Contrôlée* classification (the least prestigious classification) tends to be more expensive than one might expect.

Fashion also plays an important role in the demand (and thus the price) of a given wine. The famous "First Great Growths" of Bordeaux command fabulous prices, as millionaire wine connoisseurs vie with each other to serve these famous names. They are usually superb, but are they really worth four or five times the price of similar wines, possibly grown only a few hundred yards from the walls of the great estates?

If you have any questions, or are not sure why the prices of two wines differ, you can always ask the owner of the store or any experienced sales help. Most people coming into the store really don't know very much about wine and are rarely able to ask the sort of knowledgeable questions that gain credibility. You should not have any difficulty in establishing this credibility, and even if you are not buying today, they know that you will be back when you are ready to buy.

The purpose of this step is for you to look at a large number of bottles side by side. This will give you a chance, at no risk or expense, to familiarize yourself with different wines and the prices normally charged for them.

The Look, Listen and Learn process should continue indefinitely, every time that you visit a wine store. As you become more expert, you will be looking for different things. We always look around any wine store, even when we know what we intend to buy.

We look to see whether one of the wines we are interested in is not in fashion at that store and can be picked up inexpensively. We watch to see how the new vintages are priced and which new wines are being introduced by the producers we like. We like to see how much the prices of older vintages are going up, as the wines become better (and more scarce). We are amused to see how rarely the prices come down again, even after the wine is over the hill and barely drinkable.

## *Try, Taste and Test*

The try, taste and test part of the process is the most important part of the entire process and the most enjoyable!

Some people have the impression that there is such a thing as a perfect wine, an ideal that all wines strive to reach. This, of course, is not the case, and the quality and desirability of a certain wine can only be judged against that of other wines.

It is very difficult to evaluate one wine by itself, and the key is to compare wines that are quite similar, and to look for the differences. This is best achieved by having several wines at the table at the same time and tasting each one in turn. This is what is known as a "wine tasting". Most people feel that wine tastings are "too expensive" or "for wine experts only".

This is not true at all, and comparing different wines, one against another, is the crucial step necessary to become comfortable with different wines. Of course, many of the wine tastings you hear about are arranged by the wine trade or by acknowledged experts, and may be rather expensive.

What we have in mind are less formal and can easily be performed by anyone at home. It is less expensive (and more fun) if you can find a few friends with similar interests to share the cost.

The comparisons of the wines can be made over a meal, with two or more wines served with each course. Alternatively, you can have a slightly more formal wine tasting without going to the trouble of preparing a meal.

We have done both, and we have found that having the wine tasting with a meal works well when you are trying to compare only two wines with each course. A very good time to try this is when five or six people are in a restaurant, and everybody wants the same type of wine. Instead of ordering two bottles of the same wine, you can order two different wines, and ask for two glasses per person.

If you have more than two wines we find that a straight

wine tasting is more effective. In this case you should have some bread and some mild cheese to clean the palate between wines. You should also have some water available for the same purpose, particularly if you are going to switch between different types of wine.

It is often useful to go back and taste again a wine that has already been tasted, to compare it directly against a new one. For this reason, one or two glasses per person is definitely not enough. If you cannot borrow some glasses, it is a good idea to ask each person to bring one glass for each wine to be tasted. Alternatively, if this is not practical, you can use clear plastic tumblers, which are satisfactory for all but the most expensive wines.

The order in which you taste the wines is important. In the specific tastings we suggest for the Wine Appreciation Course at the end of this chapter, we have listed the wines in the order in which they should be drunk. This order conforms to the general rule that if you are drinking similar wines, you should drink the best and most complex wines last.

If you are drinking different types of wine, you should follow the order listed below since the palate becomes jaded as the wines become sweeter (or more complex). This applies both to wine tastings and also whenever more than one wine will be served with a meal.

If you think about it, similar rules are usually applied to the order in which food is served; a delicate fish would not normally follow a spicy Mexican chili!

> Dry before Sweet;
> White before Red;
> Light before Full-Bodied; and
> Young before Old.

Thus, you should finish all the dry wines (even if they are red, full-bodied and old) before any of the sweet wines; all the dry white wines should be drunk before the red wines, all the light red wines before the full-bodied red wines, the youngest of which should be drunk before the older and mellower ones. Sweet wines should always come at the end.

You should evaluate each wine you drink using the procedure and the criteria described in Chapter 5. Since memory is fickle, we suggest that you keep scorecards for each wine, similar to those described in the next section of this chapter.

The Wine Appreciation Course consists of specific recommendations for the types of wine you should try. In order to allow you to start at the right level for you, it is in three parts, Introductory, Intermediate, and Advanced.

Although the procedures are the same at each level, the more advanced the level, the more subtle will be the differences between the wines you are comparing. Thus, for the Introductory tastings, we assume no knowledge of wine, and the purpose of these tastings is to show you that there are differences between different wine types.

The purpose of the Intermediate wine tastings is to allow you to compare different wines that have somewhat similar characteristics, but are still sufficiently different that you should easily be able to detect differences in quality and styles. At this point you should have a reasonably clear idea of the wines that you like and first hand experience of what to look for in any wine.

The purpose of the Advanced tastings is to introduce you to the really subtle variations between different examples of the wines that you have identified as being those that you like. As you become more expert, you may actually find that the cost of drinking fine wines can actually decrease! You will be in a position to experiment with confidence and to find really superior wines, without paying the price for the "big name."

It is not necessary for you to undertake all of these tastings in order to become expert in the wines that interest you. The course is structured to help you first decide which wines you like, and then to become as expert as you wish in these wines. You can focus your efforts without going to the trouble and expense of tasting wines that do not interest you.

You should first select the color of the wine that you wish to start with. Suppose that you select white wines. After you have done the Introductory tasting for white wine, you will probably find that you like one particular type, Chardonnay wines, for example.

At this point, you can bypass all of the other Introductory Tastings, and move straight to the Intermediate Tasting number 5, "White Burgundy and Chablis types". This tasting includes several wines made from the Chardonnay grape, and you will rapidly develop a reasonably sophisticated palate for this type of wine.

You will then be ready to move right along to the Advanced Tastings for Burgundy type wines! You can, for example, try a horizontal tasting of several different Burgundies and Chablis, to see how wines from different producers compare. Alternatively, you can try a vertical tasting of wines from the same producer from several different vintages to see how the wines differ, and how the wine changes as it ages in the bottle.

At this point, you will have become really quite expert in the finer points of white Burgundy, having performed only three or four tastings. You can follow the same procedure to reach your desired level of expertise in other wines.

Thus, the expertise that we promised you at the beginning of this book can be yours with only a small investment in time and money!

Since it is not possible for us to determine which specific wines are available in your area, we have not given you specific brand names or estates to purchase. Rather, we suggest the types of wine you should buy, and leave the specific wines up to you. You should not have any difficulty in finding what you need.

In general, when you are faced with two or more examples of a type of wine we recommend, you should buy as expensive an example as you can. The more expensive wines are usually made better, and are more likely to show the characteristics you are looking for.

## *Relish, Remember and Write*

We have suggested a three pronged attack on learning to appreciate wine. The first step is to look at as many wine labels as possible. The second step is to taste and evaluate different wines with specific objectives at each stage. This third step is to make sure that you get the maximum benefit from each drop of wine that you drink, whether it be during a special wine tasting occasion, or simply having some wine at home or with friends.

Whenever you are drinking any wine, make sure that you taste and evaluate it carefully. You do not have to make a big ceremony out of the important first sip, but you can learn all you need to learn rather quickly.

You should also take a good look at the bottle and inspect the label closely. We have already suggested the things that you should look for, so we will not repeat them here. However, unlike the situation in a wine store, you can now taste the wine you are looking at and can quickly see whether it tastes the way it should.

It is a useful habit to carry in your wallet or purse a 3″ x 5″ scorecard similar to the one described below. We find that the use of this card is invaluable in making sure that we look at every wine in a systematic fashion. Writing down our evaluation helps to fix our impressions in the memory.

The scoring for the various quality-related factors were fully described in Chapter 5, so are not repeated here. The description of the wine, available from the label, and some other information that we have found to be helpful appears on the top part of the card. A description of the card and the terms used is shown below:

## WINE APPRECIATION CARD

Vintage _____ Date _____

Wine Name _____ Type _____
Producer _____ Importer _____
Occasion _____

| | | |
|---|---|---|
| Appearance (1) ___ | Color (1) ___ | Aroma (4) ___ |
| Vinegar (1) ___ | Sweet (2) ___ | Acidity (2) ___ |
| Astringent/Bitter (2) ___ | Body (1) ___ | Flavor (1) ___ |
| Finish (3) ___ | General (2) ___ | Total (20) ___ |

Comments _____

*Vintage* (if known): The year the grapes from which the wine was made were harvested.

*Date*: The date you tasted the wine. This is not necesary, but we find it helpful to see how old the wine was when we tasted it.

*Type*: The type of wine (grape varietal, official classification —Commune or Estate etc.).

*Producer*: The firm that produced and bottled the wine.

*Importer*: The firm that imported the wine.

*Occasion*: What you were doing when you tasted the wine. This is not necessary, but we find that we can remember a wine better if we are reminded of the occasion, a wedding anniversary or whatever, when we had the wine.

## Wine Appreciation Course

The following charts list the wines that should be compared together for each wine tasting. You should always try to get wines of approximately the same age. Ask for the wines as they are shown in capital letters; explanations and alternatives are shown in parentheses.

*Introductory Tastings.* During the Introductory tastings you should focus on the different tastes and aromas of the wines you are tasting. By doing this, you will begin to identify the differences between different wine types and to develop your own preferences.

We have deliberately not included in the Introductory tastings any generic wines such as California "Burgundy". Thus, each wine that we recommend should have its own clearly identifiable characteristics.

1. *Basic Red Wines*
    BEAUJOLAIS (French only: Gamay grape varietal)
    VALPOLICELLA or BARDOLINO (Italian)
    ZINFANDEL (California)
    BARBERA (Italian or California)
    PINOT NOIR (French BURGUNDY or California)
    CABERNET SAUVIGNON (BORDEAUX or California)

2. *Basic White Wines*
    SOAVE (Italian)
    CHENIN BLANC (California or VOUVRAY—French)
    SAUVIGNON BLANC or SEMILLON (California or WHITE BORDEAUX)
    RIESLING (German RHINE or MOSEL—not late picked—or California)
    (PINOT) CHARDONNAY (French BURGUNDY or French CHABLIS or California)

3. *Rosé Wines*
    ROSE DE PROVENCE (French)

PORTUGUESE ROSE (Any Brand)
GRENACHE (California)
ROSE D'ANJOU (French)
TAVEL (French)

4. *Sparkling Wines*
VIN MOUSSEUX (VOUVRAY or other French Loire)
SEKT (German sparkling wine)
NEW YORK STATE CHAMPAGNE (Champagne Method)
CALIFORNIA CHAMPAGNE (Champagne Method)
FRENCH CHAMPAGNE
ASTI SPUMANTI (Italian)

*Intermediate Tastings.* The Introductory tastings were designed to give you a reasonable idea of the types of wine you like and wish to examine further. You should now select those wines you enjoy and start to identify the quality factors you should be looking for. The wines for each of these tastings have distinct similarities, and you should be focusing on these similarities as well as on the differences between each wine.

In addition, you should concentrate on each of the important quality characteristics for each wine. When you have tasted a particular category of wines, you will have developed quite a sophisticated palate, and will be able to identify and evaluate similar wines in the future.

We have included some generic wines in these tastings, so that you can compare them with the varietal wines that they are supposed to be imitating.

5. *White Burgundy and Chablis Types*
AMERICAN "CHABLIS"
CALIFORNIA PINOT CHARDONNAY
FRENCH BURGUNDY
FRENCH CHABLIS
MEURSAULT (or other French Burgundy commune)

6. *White Rhine Types*
AMERICAN "RHINE"

LIEBFRAUMILCH (German)
CALIFORNIA RIESLING
VIN D'ALSACE (French Riesling)
RHINE (RIESLING—German, not late-picked)
MOSEL (RIESLING—German, not late-picked)
RHINE (SPATLESE or AUSLESE; Sweet)

7. *White Bordeaux Types*
AMERICAN "SAUTERNE"
FRENCH TABLE WINE (*Vin Ordinaire*)
CALIFORNIA SAUVIGNON BLANC or SEMILLON
WHITE BORDEAUX (French)
GRAVES or ENTRE-DEUX-MERS (French)
SAUTERNES (French; Sweet)

8. *Other White Wines*
ITALIAN SOAVE
DUCHESS (or other New York State varietal)
SYLVANER (German RHINE or French ALSACE)
CHENIN BLANC (California)
SANCERRE (or VOUVRAY or other French Loire)
MUSCADET (French)
ORVIETO (Italian)

9. *Light Red Wines*
AMERICAN "BEAUJOLAIS"
FRENCH TABLE WINE (Vin Ordinaire)
CALIFORNIA GAMAY
VALPOLICELLA (Italian)
BARDOLINO (Italian)
FRENCH BEAUJOLAIS
CHIANTI (Italian—not *Vecchio* or *Riserva*)

10. *Red Burgundy Types*
AMERICAN "BURGUNDY"
PINOT NOIR (California)
GAMAY BEAUJOLAIS (California varietal)

FRENCH BURGUNDY (*Appellation Bourgogne Contrôlée*)
POMMARD (or other French Burgundy commune)

11. *Red Bordeaux Types*
AMERICAN "CLARET"
CABERNET SAUVIGNON (Chile, Argentina etc.)
FRENCH BORDEAUX (*Appellation Bordeaux Contrôlée*)
CABERNET SAUVIGNON or MERLOT (California)
HAUT-MÉDOC (or other French Bordeaux commune)

12. *Other Full-Bodied Red Wines*
ZINFANDEL (California)
CATAWBA (or other New York State varietal)
CHIANTI CLASSICO (VECCHIO or RISERVA, Italian)
BAROLO or BARBARESCO (Italian)
COTES DU RHONE (or French RHONE Valley commune)
CHATEAUNEUF-DU-PAPE (French)

*Advanced Wine Tastings.* Once you have completed the Intermediate tastings, you should be confident of your wine expertise in almost any surroundings.

As you approach the Advanced tastings, we are less able to give you advice on specific wines to taste. Therefore, we are giving you the methodology used by the experts to refine their own tastes and expertise. The idea is to select wines that should be very similar, and for you to define for yourself the variable that you want to examine.

13. *Vertical Tasting*

You should select several wines from a single estate, each of which was made in a different year. Since each wine will be identical in terms of the varietal(s) used, the location of the vines, the soil conditions, the procedures used and everything else, any differences between the wines must be because the vintages are different.

This will enable you to determine the effect of bottle aging on the wine. In addition, differences in quality between two wines that are only a few years apart in age will be due to differences in the quality of the vintages.

*14. Horizontal Tasting*

Select a number of wines from the same area (e.g. Bordeaux, Napa Valley etc.) and the same vintage (and the same grape varietal if appropriate) and compare them against each other. The objective is to identify the characteristics of wines from different producers, and/or different estates, often with different official classifications.

Since all the wine is from the same vintage, differences that could be caused by different weather conditions are eliminated. Thus, this tasting will enable you to identify differences in quality between wines from different estates, communes, producers, importers or any other variable that interests you.

*15. Specialized Tastings*

At this point there are any number of tastings that you may like to try, and you should make up your own. Examples might be to try the same grape varietal from different countries; Vintage and non-vintage Champagnes from the same or from different producers; different degrees of late-picked German wines (Spätlese, Auslese, Beerenauslese, Trockenbeerenauslese), all from the same vintage and the same estate.

# 7. Quality Considerations— The French Example

All serious wine-producing countries have strict laws regarding the quality-related wording that may appear on the label of a wine bottle. The purpose of this chapter is to discuss the value of these laws to you, as a consumer, and then to take a detailed look at the laws of one country, France. The wording used in other countries is described in the chapter on each country.

We use France, not because it is the largest producer (Italy produces more wine), but because historically, French wines have been the standard against which all other wines are measured.

The French have always taken their wines very seriously, and have been willing to pay a premium for excellence. Thus the money has been available to the producers of premium wines to make the very large investments necessary to continue to make good wines.

Secondly, the French government has strictly regulated the production of wine in France for over a hundred years, and has imposed harsh penalties on those who cheat. The French wine laws have therefore become the model used by most other countries when they establish their own wine laws. As a result, once you are comfortable with the French regulations, you will have a good basis to understand the regulations of any other country.

## How Much Are Wine Labeling Laws Really Worth?

Before getting to the descriptions of the various quality classifications, it is necessary to define precisely what this protection means to you. These comments, incidentally, apply equally well to the quality classifications for German and Italian wines as well as to those for French wines. At the present time, the wine labeling laws for wines made in the U.S. are somewhat different and are described in the chapter on wines from the United States.

For a wine to carry one of the official classifications, French law requires that it be made in a certain place, using specific grape varietals, and that the winemaking method conform to the specified processes.

Although the quality classifications do guarantee these factors, there are some others that are also important, but are not guaranteed. This explains why one wine may command a price well in excess of fifty dollars, while another, which would appear to be of similar quality, only commands five dollars.

The important differences between two wines that bear the same classification are related to the location of the vineyards and to the skill, hard work, and resources of the winemaker. Making wine is an art, and there are hundreds of decisions that have to be made throughout the process. A winemaker who consistently makes good decisions will make a better wine than one who does not.

A great deal of hard work goes into the making of wine, and a winemaker who cuts corners will rarely make as good a wine as one who does everything that should be done. This is also tied into the next point, that establishing and running a good winery requires a considerable amount of money.

A well-financed winemaker will have the resources to maintain a skilled labor force, keep the vineyards in good condition and invest in the best winemaking equipment. All of these are essential if the winery is to produce superior wines.

"If this is the case," you may now ask, "a wine with a particular quality classification may be good, bad or indifferent! Why do we bother with these classifications at all?"

The reason has to do with human pride and the marketplace. The regulations have generally been defined following the methods that experience has shown must be used to produce a superior wine. Thus, all of the best wines are made using these methods, and a wine that does not use them is unlikely to be a good one.

A winemaker who does use the best techniques has the best chance of producing a good wine. He will proudly use the official term to tell the world that he has done so.

Since consumers are very label conscious, the marketplace will pay the highest prices for wines with the best quality classifications. Therefore, if the wine is entitled to use an official classification, you can be sure that the label will show it.

In conclusion, a high quality classification is not an absolute guarantee of a superior wine, but it is proof that the wine has had every chance to be good, and a wine without such a classification is unlikely to be good. Therefore, you should always buy the highest classifications that you can afford.

## Government Quality Classifications

There are certain key words on the label of all high quality French wines known as the Designation of Origin. These words are only permitted for wines that adhere to the very specific regulations for each wine. They are as follows:

*Appellation (d'Origine) Contrôlée*   The highest quality French wines all use the words *Appellation Contrôlée* or *Appellation d'Origine Contrôlée* somewhere on the label. These words may appear by themselves on the label, or the name of the wine (which is also the winemaking area) may appear between the two words, as in *Appellation Margaux Contrôlée*. Margaux is a commune in the Bordeaux region.

Strictly speaking, these words (commonly abbreviated to A.C. or A.O.C.) show that the use of the name of the place where the wine was made is "controlled". However the laws include far more than that.

For a wine to use the A.O.C. classification, it has to conform to all of the regulations that apply to it. You should note that the regulations for each particular A.O.C. classification are very specific and apply only to that particular wine. In other words, the regulations for Bordeaux wines are different from those for Burgundies. The intent is that each wine should be perfectly suited to the conditions that exist where it is made.

The principal regulations that the winemaker must respect cover the following factors:

> The winemaking region must be one that has been deemed suitable for making superior wines. A suburban garden outside Paris, for example, may not produce an A.O.C. wine. In addition, the wine must be made from grapes grown within the limits of the region.

> The wine must reach a specified percentage of alcohol; the amount of additional sugar that may be added is also regulated.

> Vine growing practices, and the maximum yield of grapes from each acre of the vineyards, are strictly regulated to control the quality of the grapes used.

> Only specific grape varietal(s) are permitted for the wines of a particular region. The winemaker is given

slight latitude in deciding the percentages of each varietal used for those wines for which some blending is allowed.

The actual processes used to make each wine are regulated to ensure some consistency in all the wines using the name of the region.

If any of the above regulations are broken, the entire production will lose its A.O.C. classification. They are occasionally "bent" a little, but serious breaches are rare.

Most winegrowing regions in France (and in Germany) are also divided into smaller winegrowing districts which, in turn, may be divided into communes. These communes, usually named after the major town or village, are relatively small geographic areas containing a number of estates. The A.O.C. laws permit wines made from grapes grown entirely within these districts and communes to use the name of the smaller area if they qualify. The smaller the A.O.C. area, the stricter are the regulations, and the better should be the wine!

If this seems complicated, perhaps an example will help. The Bordeaux region of France is divided into 21 winegrowing districts, one of which is the Haut-Médoc. The Haut-Médoc district is, itself, divided into a half-dozen communes, one of which is Pauillac. Two of the five famous "First Great Growth" (*Premier Grand Cru Classé*) wines of Bordeaux are located in the Pauillac Commune.

If an estate is located within a commune, but does not carry the communal appellation, you should be careful, since this tells you that the wine was not made in accordance with the strict communal regulations. For example, the lowest grade of A.O.C. wine made in Pauillac will merely be allowed to call itself "Bordeaux" (*Appellation Bordeaux Contrôlée*).

If it conforms to the higher standards for the Haut-Médoc, but does not conform to the even higher standards for the Pauillac appellation, it will use the words *Appellation*

*Haut-Médoc Contrôlée*. Only if it conforms to the highest standards of all, may the wine legally be called *Appellation Pauillac Contrôlée*.

Thus, a wine entitled "Pauillac" should be, and usually is, better than one called "Haut-Médoc," which, in turn, should be better than one called simply "Bordeaux". As a result, Pauillacs are generally more expensive than Haut-Médocs, which are usually more expensive than plain Bordeaux wines.

If ever you find pricing of some wines that do not follow this logic, you should be very careful. If a Pauillac is less expensive than a Haut-Médoc you have a warning that all may not be well with the Pauillac. The chances are good that the proprietor knows that the wine has turned, and perhaps you should stay away from it.

With the increasing emphasis in the U.S. on labeling wines with the grape varietal used, we are beginning to see French wines, often from Bordeaux and Burgundy, with the name of the varietal displayed, often more prominently than anything else.

The wine may or may not be good, depending on whether the words *Appellation Contrôlée* (or another quality classification) also appear. If, for example, the wine was made in Bordeaux, and these words do not appear on a bottle labeled Cabernet Sauvignon (or Sauvignon Blanc), you should not expect a good wine.

Although the wine was made using the named varietal, the wine failed to meet the A.O.C. requirements. This will usually be because the grower exceeded the production limits for his vineyard and harvested more grapes than the land could properly support. The wine will usually be thin and weak.

Of course, if the wine does carry the official classification, you may assume that the wine was properly made, and that the importer is simply marketing the wine using terms that are becoming more familiar to the sophisticated U.S. consumer.

*Vins Délimités de Qualité Supérieure (V.D.Q.S)* The second level of quality in French wines are the wines that carry the V.D.Q.S. classification. These wines are almost invariably grown in areas that are deemed to be suitable for making adequate, but not superior, wines. Alternatively, the area may be one that has only recently become involved in trying to make good wines, and the French authorities have not yet agreed that they have succeeded.

The regulations for V.D.Q.S. wines are similar to, but not as stringent as those for the A.O.C. classifications. As a result, they are frequently very well made, and because the V.D.Q.S. classification is less prestigious than the A.O.C. classification, they tend to be much less expensive.

Unfortunately, they are not widely available in the U.S., and so we could not include them in the suggested wine tastings. When they are available, however, we have generally found them to be very good value for the money.

Most of the V.D.Q.S. regions are located in the southern part of France, where the temperature is warmer, and the grapes are sweeter. Most V.D.Q.S. wines tend to be light tasting, although often rather high in alcohol.

*Vin de Pays (V.P.)* The V.P. classification was recently instituted by the wine-producing countries in the European Common Market. Most European consumers do not drink expensive wine every day, and this classification is to provide some standards for the wines that they do drink every day.

The intent is to provide a standard classification for good wines that are less expensive than those in the superior official classification, and better than the virtually unregulated table wines. The German equivalent is Landwein, and in Italy it is called Vino Tipico.

In order to get a V.P. classification, these wines have to pass a taste test of experts. In addition, they have to conform to the regulations for the making of the wine, although these are less strict than for the higher quality classifications.

Since these classifications are so new, there has been little opportunity to judge them. The first indications are encouraging, however, and it is likely that many of the truly inferior table wines imported from France and other European countries will be driven from the marketplace, to be replaced with good quality Vins de Pays.

*Vin de Table* (Table wine)   The lowest quality wine from France does not have any specific wording on the label to show that it is *Vin de Table*, commonly known as *Vin Ordinaire* (ordinary wine). Rather, the absence of any higher classification warns you not to expect much from the wine.

The French drink *Vin Ordinaire* every day, and many of these wines can be very pleasant, particularly those from reputable winemakers. However, there are very few guarantees that come with the wine, and these are primarily that the liquid was made from fermented grape juice.

The only advice we can give you is that since these wines are rarely expensive, there is no reason not to experiment a little. Unless you are lucky first time, the first few wines you buy may well not be to your liking, but if you persevere, you should soon come across one you like for everyday drinking.

# 8. The Wines of Bordeaux

## Introduction

The Bordeaux region is about 300 miles southwest of Paris, almost on the Atlantic coast. As seems to be the case so often, the best winemaking districts are on, or close to, one of three major rivers, the Dordogne, the Isle, and the Gironde. That is enough geography, and we will get on to the wine!

Bordeaux is primarily known for its world-famous red wines, which are often called "Claret" by the English. These are among the finest full-bodied red wines to be found anywhere. However, Bordeaux also produces fine dry white wines, and the extraordinary sweet white wines of Sauternes.

A wine from this area may be called Bordeaux, or it may use one of the district or communal appellations discussed in the previous chapter, if it was made following the regulations for that particular type of wine. Since the better wines do not use the name "Bordeaux" anywhere on the label, it is sometimes difficult to know whether a particular wine is from Bordeaux or from somewhere else.

For this reason, the table at the end of this chapter lists each of the districts approved by the French authorities, together with the classified communes of the Haut-Médoc. If you see any of these names on the label of an A.O.C. wine, you will know that the wine is from the Bordeaux region, using the approved Bordeaux grape varietals and winemaking methods.

It is useful to try to remember these names, but the table is rather long, and it is easy to forget. In this case, there are two other methods that you can use to help you.

The first is the shape of the bottle. The next time that you are in a wine store, take a look at several bottles of French wines that come from different regions. You will notice that wines from Bordeaux (and most Cabernet Sauvignon wines from other countries as well) have a characteristic shape, with very sharply angled "shoulders".

The second thing to look for is the name and location of the producer. Most producers of Bordeaux wines make and bottle the wine in the Bordeaux area, which is located in the Gironde department (like a U.S. state) of France. If the bottle is the right shape, and you see the word "Gironde" after the name of the producer, the chances are good that the wine is a Bordeaux, even if the A.O.C. name is unfamiliar to you.

You will sometimes see the words *Bordeaux Supérieur*. This means that the wine has 1% more alcohol than a normal Bordeaux, not that it is necessarily any better than a wine without this word.

A good red Bordeaux should be a deep red, almost purple. As it ages, a touch of brown enters the wine, and the amount of brown in the wine can be used to tell you how mature the wine is.

The aroma should be strong, and clearly characteristic of the Cabernet Sauvignon grape. The taste should be bone dry, powerful and complex, and should also demonstrate the character of this grape.

Young red Bordeaux wines will always be somewhat sharp, but this can be softened by decanting the wine and allowing it to breathe. The finish should be powerful, long lasting and without any trace of bitterness.

A good white Bordeaux should be a light, slightly golden, yellow, with no trace of brown. The aroma and the taste should be fresh and clean, with the character of the Sauvignon

Blanc or Semillon grapes from which it was made. The taste should be dry, with a hint of fruitiness, and with no sharpness or bitterness. The finish will be somewhat short lived, but be light and refreshing.

A good sweet white Bordeaux, made only in the Sauternes (and Barsac) districts should have a deep golden color, a very pronounced and fruity aroma and clearly display the character of the Semillon grape. It should be somewhat more viscous (like heated up honey) than other white wines, and the taste is sweet and pronounced. The finish should be long lasting and powerful.

## *Grape Varietals*

The full-bodied red wines of Bordeaux are made primarily from the Cabernet Sauvignon grape, although it is often blended with juice from its "cousins" the Merlot and Cabernet Franc grapes. Some districts, such as Saint-Emilion, permit the Merlot to be the primary varietal.

The Cabernet Sauvignon grape has a very strong characteristic aroma and taste, and has thrived in many other countries, primarily the United States, Chile, and Spain. Wines made entirely from it are rather harsh when young, which is the reason that the Bordeaux authorities allow the Merlot grape, which is much softer, to be blended in with it.

Dry white Bordeaux are made primarily from the Sauvignon Blanc and the Semillon grape varietals, with some Muscadelle (not to be confused with the Muscadet, used in the Loire Valley) sometimes added. White Bordeaux type wines are now also being made in the United States, sold under the Semillon and Sauvignon Blanc varietal labels.

The sweet white wines of Sauternes (and Barsac—less well known, and usually better value) are made from the Semillon grape which is left on the vine until the grapes are attacked by mould. Although the grapes look very unattractive, this mould, called *pourriture noble* (noble rottenness!") in French, is actually beneficial.

The mould breaks the skin of the grapes, and much of the water in the grape is allowed to evaporate naturally before the grapes are picked. There is only about one drop of highly concentrated liquid left in each shriveled berry when it is picked (each grape is picked by hand!).

This highly concentrated liquid is so sweet that even when the yeast stops fermenting the sugar into alcohol, there is still a lot of natural sugar left in the wine. The resulting wine is very sweet and remarkably powerful.

In order for this mould to thrive, the grapes must be picked very late in the season, so the producer runs a high risk that the weather will turn, and the crop will be ruined. In addition, making this wine is also very labor intensive. As a result, these sweet white wines are always very expensive.

Some California producers also make a wine labeled "Sauterne". This wine is not made in the same way, and is usually a dry, blended, generic wine. Please note the absence of an 's' at the end of the California name, unlike the French wine, Sauternes (with an 's' at the end).

*Vintages*

The weather in the Bordeaux region is among the most variable of any major winegrowing area in the world. As a result, the quality of the red wines of this area can vary from undrinkable to outstanding. Therefore, the vintage is among the more important criteria you use when selecting a red wine from Bordeaux. It is often even more important than drinking the wine as old as possible.

The vintage table below lists the vintages of Bordeaux since 1970 and gives an indication of how the wines were to drink, as of early 1983. The numbers, from one to five, with five as the best, indicate the quality of the vintage as a whole.

*Recent Vintages -- Red Bordeaux*

| Year | 70 | 71 | 72 | 73 | 74 | 75 | 76 | 77 | 78 | 79 | 80 | 81 |
|---|---|---|---|---|---|---|---|---|---|---|---|---|
| Rating | 4 | 3 | 1 | 2 | 3 | 4 | 2 | 1 | 5 | 4 | 3 | 4 |

*Other Good Vintages:* 1966, 1961, 1959, 1955, 1945

Since full-bodied red wines improve with age, they should be drunk as old as is reasonably possible. Thus, you would expect that a 1977 Bordeaux would be preferable to one made in 1980.

However, in Bordeaux, the differences between vintages can be so significant, that this is no longer true. The 1977 vintage was so awful that we would strongly recommend that you drink the 1980 wine today, even though 1980 was not, itself, a spectacular year.

Thus, if you have a choice between two vintages that are given a rating of three or better on the chart, you should usually go with the older vintage. However if the older wine is rated at two or one, you should buy the younger and better vintage.

The full-bodied red wines of Bordeaux are among the most long lived in the world; they remain at their peak for much longer than the red wines of Burgundy, for example. The best vintages will last for twenty or thirty years. The ordinary vintages should be drunk within about fifteen to twenty years.

The dry white Bordeaux wines derive some benefit from being aged for about three or four years. Generally speaking, the quality of the vintages for white wines is usually similar to that of the red wines, but the vintage is less important than for the red wines since the difference between white wines of different vintages is relatively subtle.

The sweet white wines of Bordeaux age very gracefully in the bottle, and should, ideally, be drunk between ten and twenty years old. Since these wines can only be made in good years anyway, age is more important than the vintage itself.

## *Appellation Contrôlée Classifications*

With few exceptions, the best Bordeaux wines are generally the Estate Bottled wines that are also entitled to carry the name of one of the districts, rather than simply being called "Bordeaux". The better Haut-Médoc wines will carry the name of the specific commune. These are shown in the table at the end of this chapter.

The best Estate Bottled wines come from estates that have been classified as superior by the French authorities. Farther on in this chapter we will show you how to identify these wines.

Estate bottled wines are entitled to use the words *Mise en Bouteille(s) au Château* or *Mise au Château*. Individual estate(s) are called château(x) in Bordeaux, although few of them are truly "castles".

The next quality level are the Estate wines that were made entirely from the grapes of one estate, but the wine was not made or bottled there. There is a unique system in Bordeaux that allows a producer to buy the grapes from an estate, make the wine elsewhere, and still call the wine by the name of the *château* where the grapes were grown.

In this case, the wine label will have the name of the *château* prominently displayed, but cannot use the very specific "Estate Bottled" wording defined above. Instead you will see the words *Mise en Bouteilles dans nos Chais,* or something similar.

Those who do not speak French are often trapped into thinking that the wine is a superior *Château* Bottled wine. These words actually mean that the wine was bottled at the producer's winery! Although the wine may be very good, these words on the label are clearly not an indication of quality, since the same can be said for any wine, including the cheaper blends from many vineyards.

The next best wines are those which are entitled to carry the name of the district. Finally come the wines that are merely entitled to be called "Bordeaux," and which may be a blend of wines grown anywhere in the Bordeaux region.

Bordeaux producers often purchase grapes from many growers, and blend them to produce wines that they sell under their own names. If the wines conform to the regulations for a particular communal or district appellation, they are entitled to use the appropriate official classification.

Some of these are quite good wines, most are rather undistinguished. Few are superior wines, since the tradition in Bordeaux, unlike that of Burgundy or Champagne, is for all of the better wines to be Estate Bottled.

## The Producer

It is reasonable to wonder why some Estate Bottled district or communal wines command prices in the hundreds of dollars, while others can be purchased for under ten dollars. The answer, of course, as we mentioned in the last chapter, is that the skill, hard work and resources of the individual estate owners differ greatly, as do the price and quality of their wines.

Does this mean that you have to try to learn the names of hundreds of *châteaux* in order to select a Bordeaux wine? It certainly helps if you can remember the names of the wines that have pleased you, so that you can choose them again. This will be easier if you always write down your opinions of every wine that you drink, as we suggested in Chapter 6.

However, this will not help you when you are faced with a selection of unfamiliar wines, as is often the case.

Fortunately, the French authorities have recognized the problem, and, over the years, have developed a reasonably comprehensive system of rating the outstanding estates in the better Bordeaux districts and communes. In the table at the end of this chapter these districts and communes are identified.

Despite the fact that some of these classifications are over 100 years old, the wines from the classified estates have generally maintained their superior quality.

There are two reasons for this. The first is that wines from these estates have consistently sold at premium prices, thus providing the estate owners with the resources to maintain the vineyards and wineries in excellent condition. In addition, the locations of the vineyards themselves are, by definition, favorable for making superior wines.

Therefore, when in doubt, look for a classified estate if you are intending to spend a fair amount of money on a Bordeaux. This will considerably improve your chances of getting a good wine.

The ratings all use the French words *"Cru Classé,"* meaning Classified Growth, and the *châteaux* are rated as *Grand Cru* (Great Growth), *Premier Cru* (First Growth), *Deuxième Cru* (Second Growth) and so on.

In typically French fashion, each district uses slightly different wording for the various levels, so it would appear that you would have to learn them all. Luckily (for you), there is only one key word to look for. This is the word *"Classé"* (Classified) after the word *"Cru"*.

You will sometimes see a wine from a district that has not been rated, such as Pomerol, use the words *"Grand Cru,"* which would lead you to believe that the wine came from a Classified Estate. However, only wines from estates that have been officially classified are allowed to use the word *"Classé"* after *"Cru"*.

Since only 63 wines out of many hundreds of *Médoc* wines were granted official classifications at all, even the fifth growth (*Cinquième Cru Classé*) wines are generally exceptional, and it is not really necessary to bother with the differences between the levels.

This is fortunate, because the actual level often does not actually appear on the label. Most of the winemakers in the *Haut-Médoc* simply use the words *"Grand Cru Classé"* (*Classé* is there!) rather than specifying the official first through fifth growth classifications.

Before leaving the topic of the producers, it seems worthwhile to spend a few minutes on the giants of the wine world, the five wines that were officially rated as the best in the world when the wines of Bordeaux were first rated in 1855. Although few of us can afford to drink them, these are the wines that are discussed most frequently, and we would like you to be able to join in the conversation when they do come up!

Although there are others that are as good (and as expensive), these wines have maintained their quality through the years, and they are still considered as the standard of excellence against which other wines are judged. Four are red wines and one is the best sweet Sauternes. The color of the wine and the name of the district or commune follows the name of the estate:

Château Lafite (red, Pauillac)
Château Latour (red, Pauillac)
Château Margaux (red, Margaux)
Château Haut Brion (red, Graves)
Château d'Yquem (white, Sauternes)

## *The Importer*

It is difficult to follow our normal advice that the producer is usually the most important factor in selecting a wine. Since each Château produces its own wine, there are just too many names to remember! There is, however, another guide that can be extremely helpful, and seems to work particularly well with Bordeaux wines.

Whenever we find a Bordeaux that we like, we always check to see who imported it into the United States. We have often found that when we like a wine imported by a particular firm, we also like others imported by the same firm.

Each firm imports only those wines that it believes will sell successfully, and which conform to the taste of the professional who selects the wine. Since taste is very personal, if you like a wine imported by a particular firm, your taste will probably be similar to the tastes of the person who selected it. There is a good chance that you will thus like other wines imported by the same firm.

Since the number of firms that import Bordeaux wines is relatively limited, careful attention to the name of the importer can significantly reduce the number of names you have to try to remember.

## How to Select a Bordeaux

In this chapter, we have covered the individual details to look out for, and it is now time to put it all together, to give you the best possible chance to get the best wine in your price range.

If you see a château or a producer whose name you remember favorably, get the best vintage of that wine you can afford. If you don't see any names you know, take a look at two or three wines that appear to be good, based on the vintage, the classification of the estate and the A.O.C. district or commune. In selecting the vintage, don't forget to find out about the storage conditions and get a young wine if they are poor.

If you are at a wine store, you will also see the name of the importer when you look at the bottle; in a restaurant, this information is rarely on the wine list, and you should ask to see the bottles.

You now have all the elements you need to make your final decision. The wine that you finally select should be imported by a reputable firm, and from the best vintage and the best *Appellation Contrôlée* classification that you can afford (in that order).

Whatever you finally decide, your choice can be made with confidence, and you should often be able to find a superior wine at a reasonable price. You will now be able to avoid being taken in by some of the "look-alike" labels that can fool the unwary consumer.

## Bordeaux Districts and Communes

| District (Commune) | Classified Estates (year) | Major Wine |
|---|---|---|
| *Major Districts and Communes* | | |
| The Médoc (includes Haut-Médoc) St.-Estèphe Pauillac St.-Julien Moulis Listrac Margaux | Yes (1855) | Red |
| Graves | Yes (1959) | Dry White, some Red |
| Saint-Emilion | Yes (1969) | Red |
| Sauternes | Yes (1855) | Sweet White |
| Pomerol | No | Red |
| Entre-Deux-Mers | No | White |
| Premieres Côtes de Bordeaux | No | Red |

*Smaller Districts (Mainly Red Wines, No Classified Estates)*

Blaye, Lalande-de-Pomerol, Bourg, Vayres, Fronsac, Néac, St. Macaire (white), Cérons (white), Loupiac, St. Foy, Ste. Croix-du-Mont (white), Barsac (white).

# 9. The Wines of Burgundy

*Introduction*

The Bourgogne (Burgundy) region is in the east central region of France, about 150 miles southeast of Paris. The winegrowing area is much smaller than that of Bordeaux, and it produces much less wine.

Burgundy is famous for both white wines and for full-bodied red wines. Some sparkling wines, both red and white, are also made.

Just south of Burgundy lies the Beaujolais district which is known for its light red wines, while to the northwest is the Chablis district, famous for white wines. Although neither Beaujolais nor Chablis is actually part of Burgundy, they are usually included in discussions of the wines from Burgundy.

Red and white wines are produced in all communes of Burgundy. The table at the end of this chapter shows the color that predominates in each commune. As with Bordeaux wines, if you don't remember all of these names, it can sometimes be difficult to know if a particular wine is, indeed, a Burgundy. Again, the shape of the bottle and the location of the producer can help you, as can the price of the wine!

The shape of a Burgundy bottle is not as distinctive as a Bordeaux bottle, since wines from the Rhône and Loire Valleys also use similar bottles. The bottles have long sloping shoulders as opposed to the more clearly defined shoulders of the Bordeaux bottles. They are wider and shorter than the long, thin bottles of wines from Germany and Alsace.

Most of the prestigious Burgundy producers are located in the Côte d'Or, and you will often find these words after the name of the producer. Alternatively, you will see the name of the department "Saône et Loire," also shown as "S. et L."

Finally, so little wine is produced in Burgundy, and the demand for these wines is so great, that prices for Burgundy wines are always relatively high. Thus, if you come across a relatively expensive A.O.C. wine, in a Burgundy shaped bottle, that shows one of the locations listed above, you can be sure that the wine is a Burgundy.

The full-bodied red wines of Burgundy should be a deep red, tending towards magenta (a deep pink), rather than the purple of Bordeaux. As the wine ages, it too will become slightly brownish, but not so much as an older Bordeaux. If the wine is distinctly brown, it is probably too old.

It should have a powerful fruity aroma, and show clearly the characteristics of the Pinot Noir grape varietal. The taste should be full and somewhat complex, with a strong and long lasting finish.

A recent trend in Burgundy is to make wines that mature more quickly than they used to, with the result that a young Burgundy is not usually as sharp as a young Bordeaux.

A good dry white Burgundy should have a greeny gold color and the rich and complex aroma of the Chardonnay grape varietal. Wines from Chablis tend to have a somewhat crisper flavor than the wines from farther south in Burgundy proper, although both should be fruity and absolutely dry.

The finish should be refreshing and should linger on the tongue for longer than you would expect for a dry white wine. It is this finish that distinguishes the Chablis and white Burgundies, and makes them the most copied wines in the world.

A Beaujolais should have a relatively light red color. You

should be able to see a light on the other side of the glass with no difficulty, whereas the color of a full-bodied Burgundy is generally so deep that you have to look at the top of the wine to inspect the color and the clarity.

Any hint of brown in the color of a Beaujolais means that the wine is too old. If the wine is more than three or four years old, it is not fair for you to return it, since you chose it! If, on the other hand, it is only a year or two old, a brownish tinge means that the wine was stored extremely badly, and you should send it back if it is over the hill.

The aroma of a Beaujolais is less intense than that of a red Burgundy and should be light and fruity. The taste should be fresh and uncomplicated, with almost no sharpness from the tannins. The finish should be refreshing and short lived.

## *Grape Varietals*

The powerful red wines of Burgundy are made almost entirely from the Pinot Noir grape. In Burgundy, and, so far, in Burgundy alone, this varietal produces a complex delightful wine that many believe to be the best red wine in the world.

The Pinot Noir has been planted in many other places around the world, but has not, to our knowledge, produced a wine that approaches the majesty of a great Burgundy. Eventually this will change, and a winemaker will find the right combination of soil and climate. Until this happens, however, Burgundy lovers will have to accept the scarcity and high prices that this wine commands.

The best dry white Burgundies are made from the Chardonnay grape, also known as the Pinot Chardonnay. This varietal produces the most complex of the dry white wines, and a wine that improves in the bottle for three or four years.

This grape, unlike the Pinot Noir, has taken well to other places, particularly in California. Winemakers have succeeded in making very good white Burgundy and Chablis type wines, which are usually sold under the varietal label.

Some white Burgundies are made with the Aligoté grape varietal, and are usually sold under the label *Appellation Bourgogne-Aligoté Contrôlée*. These tend to be lighter and less complex than the superior Chardonnay Burgundies.

Beaujolais wines are made from the Gamay grape which provides a delightful light red wine that many people enjoy. This grape has only enjoyed moderate success in other places.

California producers make a wine from a varietal known as the "Gamay Beaujolais," which is a mystery grape. It appears to be more closely related to the Pinot Noir than to the Gamay, and generally produces a wine that is heavier than a Beaujolais and lighter than a Burgundy. The taste and aroma are similar to both and characteristic of neither!

## Vintages

The weather in Burgundy plays an extremely important role in the quality of the red wines, has some effect on the quality of the white wines, and has less effect on the quality of the lighter wines from Beaujolais. The table below gives our judgment of the wines of the vintages from 1970 to 1981, as of early 1983. As always, this table should be used with caution, since individual wines may be better or worse than these averages.

*Recent Vintages — Red Burgundy*

| Year | 70 | 71 | 72 | 73 | 74 | 75 | 76 | 77 | 78 | 79 | 80 | 81 |
|---|---|---|---|---|---|---|---|---|---|---|---|---|
| Rating | 1 | 5 | 4 | 2 | 3 | 1 | 4 | 2 | 5 | 3 | 2 | 1 |

Red Burgundies mature more quickly than the fuller wines of Bordeaux and some of the very heavy Italian reds. The only older vintage that is still good is the 1969 vintage, and possibly some of the exceptional wines of 1961.

The poorer wines should be drunk between two and five years old (they will never get any better). The finer wines should ideally be drunk when they are between eight and about fifteen years old, with the better ones being kept for the longer periods.

The wines of Beaujolais do not age well, and should be drunk before they are three years old.

The white wines of Burgundy and Chablis improve subtly in the bottle, and the connoisseurs like to drink the better wines between three and about seven years old. Since the difference between a young and an older white wine is not significant, we suggest that all you need to remember is not to drink them too old.

## Appellation Contrôlée Classifications

The A.O.C. laws in Burgundy are easier to remember than those of Bordeaux because there is more uniformity across the whole region.

Burgundy is divided into four major areas (plus Chablis and Beaujolais). The finest wines come from the Côte de Nuits and the Côte de Beaune, which are collectively known as the Côte d'Or (the Gold Slope). The best of these wines are from the specially classified estates, each of which has its own A.O.C. appellation.

After the specially classified Estate Bottled wines come those that are named after the A.O.C. communes, followed by those that are merely entitled to use the general *Appellation Bourgogne Contrôlée* classification. As with Bordeaux, the better the classification, the stricter are the requirements.

Many communes have attached the name of a famous estate to the name of the town. For example, the town of Chambolle added the name of the Musigny estate to form the A.O.C. label of Chambolle-Musigny. Wines of Chambolle-

Musigny should not be confused with wine from the Grand Cru estate of Musigny!

The following table shows you what to look for on a Burgundy label to determine the quality level. You should note that the size of the letters used for the name of the estate and that of the commune are crucial. The best classifications are shown first.

| Classification | Description |
| --- | --- |
| *Burgundy* | |
| Grand Cru | Outstanding wines made from one of the 31 "Great Growth" estates. Only the name of the Estate is shown. Neither the words *"Grand Cru"* nor the name of the commune usually appear. They are always very expensive. |
| Premier Cru | Wine made from superior classified estates. If the name of the commune and that of the estate are displayed using the same sized letters, the wine is from a *Premier Cru* estate. |
| Commune | Wine from estates within the boundaries of the commune. They are usually blends from many vineyards. The name of the commune and that of the producer will normally be prominent. For Estate Bottled wines, the name of the estate is usually smaller than that of the commune. If the estate name is larger, the commune only appears in very small letters between *"Appellation"* and *"Contrôlée"* (as opposed to *Grand Cru* wines where the commune does not appear at all). |
| Bourgogne | Wine made from estates within the classified Burgundy region. |

*Chablis*

| | |
|---|---|
| Chablis Grand Cru | Outstanding wines from one of the seven outstanding "Great Growth" Chablis estates. |
| Chablis Premier Cru | Superior wines from selected First Growth estates. |
| Chablis | Good, but not outstanding, wines from estates within the boundaries of Chablis. |
| Petit Chablis | Lesser wines from estates within the boundaries of Chablis. These wines are rarely found in the United States. |

*Beaujolais*

| | |
|---|---|
| Cru Beaujolais | Wines from one of the nine Beaujolais communes listed in the table at the end of this chapter. There are no classified estates in Beaujolais. |
| Beaujolais Villages | Wines from estates within any of the 38 selected communes in the Beaujolais district. |
| Beaujolais Supérieur | Wines from estates within the Beaujolais district that have at least 1% more alcohol than the minimum for a normal Beaujolais. |
| Beaujolais | Wines from estates within the Beaujolais district. |
| Beaujolais Nouveau (or Primeur) | A special classification for wines made at the beginning of the harvest and which should be drunk within about three months of being made. |

## The Producer

Most estates in Burgundy are less than twenty acres, and few are large enough to warrant their own bottling facilities.

These few are generally the *Grand Cru* and *Premier Cru* estates described in the preceding section. These wines are deemed to be the best wines that Burgundy produces.

Estate Bottled wines in Burgundy will use the words *Mise (en Bouteilles) à la Propriété* or *Mise (en Bouteilles) au Domaine,* both of which mean "Bottled on the Estate". Any other wording indicates that the wine is not Estate Bottled. The term "Château" is not generally used for the classified Burgundy estates, although you will sometimes see it on some labels. The better estates generally use the terms "Domaine" or "Propriété".

Because the estates are so small, most wines are made by producers who select grapes from many vineyards within the boundaries of the various communes and blend them for sale under the communal appellation. The name of the producer is usually displayed prominently, as is that of the communal. This is the next level of quality.

These wines generally represent the best value for your money. The problem, however, is to find out which producers make good wines. If there were many of these producers, as there are in Bordeaux, where each estate is its own producer, the task would be very difficult.

Fortunately, there are only relatively few producers, and those that make good wines from one commune usually make equally good wines from others. You should remember the name of the producer whenever you find a good (or poor) Burgundy, and try (or avoid) other wines from the same house.

The lowest level of quality are those wines that are simply entitled to be called *Appellation Bourgogne Contrôlée*. These wines have been made from the grapes from estates in many communes or have not been made in accordance with the stricter requirements for the communal appellation.

However, the better producers in Burgundy also make very acceptable wines in this class and you will usually get a decent wine, at a price that reflects the A.O.C. level.

## The Importer

We suggested that you try to remember the names of the firms that imported good and poor wines from Bordeaux to guide you for future purchases.

For Burgundy, the name of the importer, while helpful, is less useful as a guide than the name of the producer. Since there are only a few Burgundy producers whose wines are available in the U.S., it is more effective to focus your efforts on remembering the name of the producer rather than that of the importer.

## How to Select a Burgundy

If your budget runs to the Estate Bottled *Grand* or *Premier Cru* wines, these are obviously the ones to go for. For most people, however, these are rather too expensive. However, unlike Bordeaux, (where all of the best wines are Estate Bottled), the communal wines of Burgundy are excellent, provided that the wine was made by one of the better producers.

Whenever you buy a red or white Burgundy, again we recommend that you write down your impressions of the wine, and remember the name of the producer. Once you have selected one or more producers whose wine you like, select a communal wine of a vintage that has every chance of being good. If you do not see the name of any producer that you recognize, all you can do is to take a chance on one of them, and remember the name for the next time.

The same approach should be used for buying a Beaujolais, although in this case we have sometimes found that the classification is as important as the name of the producer. In other words, any *Cru* Beaujolais will probably be better than a wine simply entitled "Beaujolais," regardless of the producer.

## Burgundy Communes

*Côte de Nuits:* (The best red wines, powerful and slow maturing; a few good white wines.)
    Fixin (red)
    Gevrey-Chambertin (red)
    Morey-Saint-Denis (red)
    Chambolle-Musigny (red; some white)
    Vougeot (red and white)
    Vosne-Romanée (red)
    Echézeaux (red)
    Nuits-Saint-Georges (red; some white)

*Côte-de-Beaune:* (The best white wines, fragrant and full of flavor; fine, quicker maturing red wines.)
    Prémeaux (red)
    Pernand-Vergelesses (red)
    Corton (red and white)
    Aloxe-Corton (red and white)
    Savigny (red)
    Beaune (red)
    Pommard (red)
    Volnay (red)
    Meursault (white; some red)
    Auxey-Duresses (red)
    Puligny-Montrachet (white)
    Chassagne-Montrachet (white)
    Santenay (red; some white)

*Côte Chalonnais:* (Lighter red wines, medium-bodied white wines; sparkling Burgundies.)
    Rully (red and white)
    Mercurey (red)
    Givry (red and white)
    Montagny (white)

*Mâcon:* (Light, crisp white wines.)
    Pouilly-Fuissé (white)
    Pouilly-Loché (white)
    Pouilly-Vinzelles (white)
    St.-Véran (white)
    Viré (white)

*Beaujolais:* (Light, crisp red wines; a little white wine.)
- St.-Amour
- Juliénas
- Chénas
- Moulin-à-Vent
- Fleurie
- Chiroubles
- Morgon
- Côte de Brouilly
- Brouilly

*Chablis:* (Dry, full-bodied, crisp white wines.)
- No A.O.C. communes

# 10. The Wines of Champagne and Other French Wines

## Champagne

*Introduction*

The Champagne winemaking region is in the northeast of France, about 40 miles east of Paris. Its white sparkling wines are known the world over. Some red and still white wines are also made, but their appeal is limited. In addition, some producers make a rosé Champagne (called "pink" Champagne in English), which is of interest primarily for its visual effect.

France also produces other sparkling wines (called *Vins Mousseux*), but only wines made from the specified varietals grown within the boundaries of the Champagne A.O.C. region may be called "Champagne". In addition, the wine must be made according to the procedure laid down by French law and known as the *Méthode Champenoise*, the "Champagne Method" described farther on in this chapter.

The word "Champagne" has limited protection in the U.S., and you will often see sparkling wines, made in countries other than France, also called "Champagne". Some are good, others less so.

A good Champagne is a pale golden color, and has a somewhat grapy aroma and taste. The best Champagnes are dry, although some are made to be noticeably sweet. The finish should be fresh and clean, without lasting very long on the palate.

When the bottle is opened, the cork should come out with a good pop. The bubbles should be very small and should remain in the wine until it has all been drunk.

## *Grape Varietals*

Champagne is a blended wine usually made from the juice of both red and white grape varietals. If the wine is made entirely from white grapes it may be called *"Blanc de Blancs"*. This is is not an indication of quality, but merely indicates the style of the wine.

The grapes used are, surprisingly to many, the same varietals used to make the majestic wines of Burgundy. The red grape is the Pinot Noir and the white grape is the Chardonnay. Equally surprisingly, these grapes do not make good still wines in the Champagne region. This is because the Champagne vineyards are so much farther north, and thus cooler, than those of Burgundy.

When white Champagne is being made from the Pinot Noir, the skins of the grapes are removed immediately after pressing, so that none of the pigmentation from the skins enters the wine.

Pink Champagne is made either by blending red and white wines, or by leaving the skins of the red grapes in the fermenting grape juice until just enough of the color has entered the wine to produce the desired result.

In either case, there is a considerable risk that the wine will not come out the way it should. For this reason, pink Champagne is usually priced at a premium. Since the taste and other qualities are very similar to the normal white Champagne, you should only pay this premium if you particularly want a pink wine.

## Vintages

Champagne is usually a blend of wines from different vintages. Most producers try to produce Champagnes that are consistent in style and taste from year to year, regardless of the weather in any particular year.

In order to achieve this, they usually blend wines from better years with those from years when the weather was less favorable. As a result, most Champagne is called "non-vintage," and you do not have to try to remember the good and bad years.

The weather in some years is particularly favorable and produces a superior wine. When this happens, the producer declares a "Vintage Year," and makes a Champagne entirely of the grapes of that harvest. This wine is sold as vintage Champagne.

Since the supply is limited, vintage Champagne sells at a significant premium over non-vintage Champagne, even though most non-vintage Champagne contains enough wine from the good years to produce an excellent wine. Although vintage Champagnes are unquestionably better, we feel that the difference in quality rarely justifies the additional money.

Champagne, if it is well stored, will improve in the bottle for a year or so. It should generally be drunk within the next two or three years. One of the dangers of non-vintage Champagne is that you do not know when it was made. When in doubt, you should ask the proprietor how long it has been in stock. The one advantage of drinking vintage Champagne is that, at least, you know its age!

## Appellation Contrôlée Classifications

Champagne is the one classified region in France that does not require the words "*Appellation Contrôlée*" anywhere on the label. Any French wine with the word "Champagne" on the label must have conformed to the laws relating to the types and origins of the grapes, and the methods used in the production of this wine.

Since Champagne is usually a blend of grapes from different estates, there are no Estate Bottled Champagnes, nor are there any classified estates. The Champagne region is not even divided into districts or communes! Thus, you only have to look for the word "Champagne" (and the vintage if you are looking for a vintage Champagne).

The label does, however, tell you how sweet the wine will be. The following terms are used on the labels of all French sparkling wines (not only Champagne).

*Brut* — this is the dryest Champagne;
*Extra Sec* (Extra Dry) — this is much less dry;
*Sec* (Dry) — this is actually rather sweet!
*Demi-Sec*, or *Doux* (Half-Dry, or Soft) — this is very sweet, and is rarely found in the U.S.

## *La Méthode Champenoise (the Champagne Method)*

The main reason that Champagne costs so much is that it is very expensive to make. The major steps that go into the production of Champagne are summarized below:

1. The grapes are harvested, crushed, and allowed to ferment.

2. The wine is then blended with wines from different vintages and other estates to achieve the standard taste and aroma that characterize the Champagnes of the producer. Vintage Champagnes are blended only with other wines from the same year.

3. When the wine is bottled, a small amount of additional sugar and yeast is added. The bottle is firmly sealed with a temporary cork. The wine then ferments a

second time in the bottle, and the added sugar is converted to alcohol and carbon dioxide gas. This gas cannot escape, and dissolves in the wine to come out as bubbles when the bottle is opened.

4. The wine is turned upside down for a year or more so that the sediment formed by the second fermentation falls to the neck of the bottle.

5. The neck of the bottle (with the sediment) is frozen. When the bottle is then opened, the frozen wine, containing the sediment, pops out. This wine is then replaced with fresh wine and/or sugar (if a sweet wine is desired), and the wine is resealed as quickly as possible.

6. The familiar wire cage is then applied to the top of the bottle to ensure that the cork does not fly out as a result of the tremendous pressure from the carbon dioxide gas.

This process is very labor intensive. Other sparkling wines are made by what is known as the "Tank Method". In this case, steps 3, 4 and 5 are omitted, and the wine is bottled under pressure. Since these are the expensive steps to perform, wines produced using the Tank Method are often less expensive than those using the Champagne Method.

## *The Producer*

The name, skill, hard work and resources of the producer are by far the most important considerations when buying Champagne. Most Champagnes display prominently, and are known by, the name of the house that produced the wine. Most producers own some vineyards, but they usually buy wines from several growers to make wines that they market under their own names.

Fortunately, only a few producers sell Champagne in the

United States, and each one tries to make an identical wine each year. You thus have to try only a few Champagnes to find one you like.

However, even if you get a wine list without a single Champagne that you recognize, the general level of French Champagne is so high that it is unusual to find one that is truly poorly made.

Some of the larger Champagne houses also produce a "premium quality" brand, which can sell for two or three times the price of the normal non-vintage Champagne produced by the same house.

This is invariably a vintage Champagne, and is usually made from the *Tête de Cuvée*, or first pressing of the grapes. The words *Tête de Cuvée* may, but do not have to, appear on the label. These wines can easily be identified by the price, which we have generally found to be excessive when the quality is compared to other Champagne from the same producer.

We suspect that most people who purchase these wines are more interested in showing that they are willing, and able, to buy "the best," than in getting good value for the money. The same is not necessarily true for paying a premium for a superb Bordeaux, for example, where there is an enormous difference between a superlative wine and one that is merely good.

Our advice is that you would do better by buying an extra bottle, or two, of non-vintage Champagne from the same producer, rather than paying a great deal more for the premium brand.

## *Other French Wines*

The regions of Bordeaux, Burgundy and Champagne produce the wines that set the standards of excellence for the rest of the world, and they have been discussed at some length.

There are many A.O.C. regions in France, but there are only three more, Alsace, the Loire and the Rhône Valley, where the quality and availability of the wines are significant. These are covered next, although in less detail than the wine from the major wine-producing regions.

## The Wines of Alsace

Alsatian wines are predominantly white and made from several grape varietals, of which the most common are the Riesling, (Gewürz) Traminer and Sylvaner. They are usually marketed in long, thin green bottles, similar to bottles used for the German Mosel wines. Alsace is located in the eastern part of France (near the German border), almost due east of Paris.

The wines are quite similar to the famous German wines (they are made from many of the same grape varietals), but they are generally lighter and less complex than the German wines. During the Second World War, the vineyards were allowed to deteriorate, with the result that Alsatian wines are not usually quite as good as the better German wines, nor are they as expensive.

The A.O.C. laws in Alsace allow the producers to use one or more varietals to make wine, and the wines will be quite different depending on the varietal(s) used. You should always look for the name of the varietal on the label, since the better wines always name the grape varietal used. If an Alsatian wine does not specify the grape, you can be reasonably certain that the wine was a blend, or made from an inferior varietal (usually the Sylvaner).

Alsace has no communes or classified estates, and most wines are blends from several estates. Some of the producers do own their own estates, and they will sell the wine under the name of the estate, usually using similar wording to that used in

Burgundy—*Mise (en Bouteilles) à la Propriété* (or *au Domaine*).

You will often see an Alsatian wine using the words "*Grand Vin*" (Great Wine), "*Réserve Exceptionelle*" (Exceptional Reserve), or some combination of "Grand" or "Reserve". These are not specific indicators of quality, but simply mean that the alcohol content of the wine is higher (a minimum of 11%) than for wines without these words.

Like Champagne, Alsatian wines are blends from different vintages, as well as from different estates. As a result, you do not have to be concerned with the vintage year, and these wines should also be drunk young.

Since the producers also try to produce wines that are consistent from year to year, you should use the same technique for wines from Alsace that we suggested for Champagnes. You should try several wines until you find a producer whose wines you like and then buy other wines made by that producer.

Good wines from Alsace should generally be a pale greeny white, with little acidity, and a reasonably strong aroma and taste—clearly characteristic of the varietal. The finish for wines made from most varietals should be fresh and clean, and will not last very long on the palate. Good wines made from the Gewürztraminer have a longer and more spicy finish (*Gewürz* is German for spicy).

## Wines from the Loire Valley

The Loire Valley, located about 100 miles southeast of Paris is the largest A.O.C. region in France. It produces large quantities of good, but rarely excellent, white and rosé wines. Most of the better Vins Mousseux (sparkling wines, not made in Champagne) are also produced in this area.

There are a great many A.O.C. districts in the Loire Valley, but most of them are relatively small, and their wines are not widely available in the United States. The most famous names you are likely to come across on any wine list, are as follows: Anjou (rosé and white), Sancerre (white), Pouilly-Fumé (white, not to be confused with Pouilly-Fuissé in Burgundy), Vouvray (white), Touraine (white, rosé and some red), Saumur (white), and Muscadet (white).

In our judgment, the best French rosé wines come from Anjou, although some argue that this honor belongs to Tavel, in the Rhône Valley (discussed in the next section). Rosé d'Anjou should not be confused with Rosé de Provence, which comes from the south of France, and which is generally a pleasant, but far from distinguished wine.

Rosé wines from Anjou are made from the red Cabernet Franc grape, and the skins are removed before the full color has been imparted to the wine. The color ranges from a purplish pink, to a wine that has so little color from the skins that it is known as *vin gris* (gray wine).

Sancerre and Pouilly-Fumé produce delightful and very dry white wines. The grape varietal used is the same Sauvignon Blanc grape grown in Bordeaux, but the more northerly climate in the Loire provides a lighter and somewhat crisper wine.

The white wines from Vouvray, Touraine, Saumur and Anjou are made from the Chenin Blanc varietal (also called Pineau de la Loire). These wines tend to be fruitier than those made from the Sauvignon Blanc in Sancerre. Also, they tend to be somewhat sweeter, although this is a fresh, natural sweetness, unlike those wines to which the sugar has been added later.

These communes also produce some fine sparkling wines, often using the Champagne method. Although, under French law, they may not be called "Champagne," they are usually very pleasant, and should often take the place of the more expensive Champagnes when snob value is not important.

Muscadet is not a place, but the name of the grape varietal. This name may only be used for wines which were made from Muscadet grapes grown in the Loire Valley and which conform to the A.O.C. requirements for this wine. The best Muscadets are entitled to use the *Sèvre et Maine* and *Côteaux de la Loire* appellations.

A good Muscadet is a golden white color, often with a touch of green. It has a light taste, slightly acidic, and a medium strong finish. The French feel that it is the best wine to accompany fish, and we don't disagree.

## *Wines from the Rhône Valley*

The most underrated major wine-producing region of France is the Rhône Valley, about 100 miles south of Burgundy. This region, with its warm climate, produces powerful, robust red wines with a high alcohol content. Some white wines are made, and one commune, Tavel, produces a well-known rosé wine.

In the nineteenth century, the better Rhône wines were rated as highly as the best Bordeaux and Burgundies. For reasons that are not entirely clear, they fell out of fashion.

As a result, the wines could no longer command the premium prices necessary to maintain the vineyards and production facilities in top notch condition. The quality of the wines then declined, prices dropped further, and the vicious circle continued.

However, as a result of the increasing interest in wine and higher prices for top-rated wines, the estates of the Rhône Valley have been upgraded, and are now producing some superb wines.

If you like full-bodied red wines, we urge you to focus on the wines of this region. They are not yet fashionable, although they will be soon, and you can get some spectacular wines at reasonable prices.

Because the Rhône Valley is inland, and toward the south of France, the weather is usually rather warm. This results in sweet grapes, and wines for which the minimum alcohol content is the highest for any A.O.C. wine in France.

The importance of the vintage for Rhône wines is somewhat controversial. However, apart from the extremes, the weather is reasonably consistent, and the wines improve enormously in the bottle. Furthermore, most Rhône wines are blends of two, or more, varietals, since most producers change the proportions of the varietals to compensate for differences in the weather from year to year.

We therefore recommend that you buy as old a full-bodied red wine as you can, without bothering too much about the vintage. Most Rhône wines throw a sediment, even when quite young. Young or old, they should always be decanted.

If possible, they should be aged for at least five years; the better wines from good vintages can be kept for twenty years or so. The high alcohol content seems to cut the sharpness of the tannin, so these wines are not unpleasant when served quite young.

The best known Rhône Valley A.O.C. districts are as follows (from north to south, which also serves as a very rough order of quality, with the best wines in the north): Côte Rotie, Hermitage, Côtes du Rhône, Châteauneuf-du-Pape, Lirac, and Tavel (rosé wines).

Wines from the Côte Rôtie and the Hermitage districts are generally considered to be the most elegant, and are made primarily from the Syrah grape varietal. These wines are usually a very deep red, again turning somewhat brown as they age. The taste and the aroma are powerful and complex, and should clearly show the character of the Syrah.

Farther south is the Côtes du Rhône itself, and the smaller communes of Châteauneuf-du-Pape and Lirac. These wines are generally rich, full-bodied red wines, although there is a tendency on the part of the producers to make lighter wines, ready for immediate consumption.

This can be done because the producers have a great deal of latitude in selecting the proportions of each grape varietal used. Many of them are blending in large amounts of the lighter Grenache varietal and even some white grapes into their wines. The label will give you no help as to the varietals used, but you can get some idea of the wine by looking at the color.

The deeper and more purple the wine, the more full-bodied and complex it should be, and the longer it should be allowed to mature. You can usually judge the color by looking at the wine before opening the bottle. If the wine is significantly paler than other full-bodied red wines, you should anticipate a light red wine and treat it as such. It should also be less expensive than a good full-bodied red wine.

The proportions of the varietals may be changed each year to compensate for differences in the weather conditions. This inconsistency in the varietals used actually helps the producer to be more consistent in the wines he makes each year, and when you find a producer whose wines you like, you can be reasonably sure that wines from other vintages will be similar.

The last Rhône wine to discuss is an anomaly in a region famous for its powerful red wines, and is the district of Tavel, which produces an excellent rosé wine from the same Grenache varietal that is producing some very fine wines in California.

Tavel rosé wines are pink in color with a hint of orange. They are very alcoholic, and are among the heavier of the rosé wines, with a strong taste, aroma and finish. Like most rosé wines, they should be drunk chilled, and within a few years of the vintage.

# 11. The Wines of Germany

*Introduction*

Germany is known primarily for its white wines, which range from average to spectacular. Some red wines are also made, but they are generally rather poor, and rarely found outside Germany. In addition, some sparkling wines, called "Sekt," are produced.

All of the major wines are made in the valleys of the Rhine and the rivers that flow into it. This area is divided into specific districts, and the wine will carry the name of the district in which it was made.

The best German wines are made from the Riesling grape varietal. These wines should be a light golden color, (often with a touch of green for Mosel wines), and should have the strong, rather fruity aroma and taste of this grape.

The normal wines should have a dry, crisp, and slightly acidic taste; the finish is strong and fruity, without being sweet or cloying. They should be served chilled, and go well with most foods, particularly with fish and poultry.

Some wines are especially designated as having been made from grapes picked late in the season, when they are riper and sweeter. These will be more golden in color and will be sweeter, with a more powerful and long-lived aroma and finish. These are the best of the German wines, and the most expensive. They, too, should be served chilled and are usually drunk alone or with dessert.

For the normal consumer, there are five major (and two minor) factors that determine the quality of a German wine. These explain why one wine may be expensive at ten dollars a bottle, while another, possibly from the same district, and even the same vintage, is a bargain at over one hundred dollars.

These are as follows (in rough order of importance, the most important first): the official classification of the wine, when the grapes were picked, the skill and resources of the producer, the importer, and the grape varietal used. Of lesser importance are the vintage and the specific district where the grapes were grown.

Fortunately, German wine labels give you the most information of any in the world, and they have recently been simplified to make them more intelligible. The next few pages tell you what to look for on the label under each of these headings.

## *Official Classifications*

In France, Italy and increasingly in the United States, the primary indicator of quality is set by the location of the vineyard(s). In other words, superior ratings are given to all wines that conform to the regulations for the specified region, district or commune, regardless of the quality of any particular vintage or batch.

The same is not true in Germany, where each and every wine has to be tested and tasted each year to determine the quality classification it will be given. Not only must the wine have conformed to the regulations, but also the actual quality rating will depend on the results of these tests.

If the wine passes the tests, it is given one of the superior ratings, and each bottle must carry the official number of the test for that particular batch. This number is shown as the

*Amtliche Prüfungsnummer* or A.P.Nr.

The reason why wines from the same estate may carry different ratings in different years is because the weather in the winegrowing areas is so variable, as is the wine. The German vineyards are so far north that the summers are sometimes not warm enough to allow the grapes to ripen properly.

In these years, the grapes are not sweet enough for the natural sugar to generate enough alcohol during fermentation to make an acceptable wine. Sugar has to be added to the grape juice, and the wines are not given the top rating.

On the other hand, in particularly good years, spectacular wines can be made! In these years, the winemaker delays picking some grapes until the last possible moment. He hopes that the same mould that attacks the grapes in Sauternes will also attack his grapes, with the same result.

When he is in luck, and the weather holds, German winemakers make sweet white wines that are as good as, or better than, any made in Sauternes. These wines are especially rated to show when the grapes were picked, and are, by far, the most important factor that you should consider when selecting a German wine. Not only do they define the quality of the wine, but they also give you an excellent indication of the character you should expect it to show.

*Tafelwein* (Table wine): This is the lowest quality of German wine, and is merely controlled to the extent that the contents of the bottle must be made from fermented grape juice and be safe to drink. There are few controls on the origin of the grapes or on the winemaking methods employed.

The word "*Tafelwein*" may, or may not appear on the label. If you do not see one of the better classifications described below, you know that the wine is a simple *Tafelwein*.

*Landwein* (Country wine): This, the first level of rated wine, has been recently been instituted in all of the European

Common Market wine-producing countries. It is intended to show that the wine has been tasted and tested, and has passed moderately strict quality standards for an everyday drinking wine.

*Qualitätswein bestimmter Anbaugebiete* (Quality wine from a designated region): This is usually abbreviated to "Qualitätswein" on the label, and to QbA when being written about, as opposed to QmP for the top-rated wines, discussed below.

QbA wines are similar in quality to the regional A.O.C. (e.g. Bordeaux) wines of France, although, they may be the best wines that could be produced by a superb estate in a poor year.

For a wine to be rated as a QbA, it must show the designated region where the grapes were grown, and the grapes must have reached a minimum degree of ripeness (and natural sugar content). In addition, the yield from the vineyard is regulated, as are the production methods used for making the wine.

Furthermore, the actual wine itself must pass the official taste and chemical tests for a QbA wine. The Prüfungsnummer must appear on the label of all wines rated QbA (or QmP).

We feel that the best values in German wines are among the QbA wines, which are rarely very expensive and usually very pleasant to drink.

*Qualitätswein mit Prädikat* (Quality wines with Honors): The finest German wines carry the QmP classification. This level is similar in quality to the better French communal appellations.

To gain a QmP classification, the wine must have been made from grapes within a single commune, and it must pass taste and chemical tests that are more stringent than those for a QbA wine; lastly, no sugar can have been added to the grape juice. In practice, QmP wines can only be made when the vintage is reasonably good.

When you buy a QmP wine, this classification gives you a better guarantee of getting a superior wine than does the label of any wine made in any other country. You know that the vintage was at least reasonable, and that the wine itself has passed the stringent quality tests.

In good years (only), a German winemaker may harvest the grapes several times, taking only the grapes that are ripe at each pass. As the autumn progresses, the grapes become riper and sweeter, and they make better wine. Thus, the same estate can make several different wines in the same year!

The wine laws take this into account, and for QmP wines only, the labels will indicate when the grapes were picked for the actual wine in the bottle. These late-picked wines represent only a tiny proportion of all the wine made, and they are usually rather expensive. The words that you may expect to find on the label are described below:

> *Kabinett:* This is the basic grade of QmP wines. The grapes have been picked at the normal time, and were sweet enough to make a good wine without the addition of sugar. They should be dry and can be drunk with food. They should be drunk within about five years.
>
> The word "*Kabinett*" may, or may not, appear. If the wine is a QmP wine, and does not have any of the late-picked classifications described below, the wine is a *Kabinett* level wine.
>
> *Spätlese:* These wines were made from grapes that were picked later than the *Kabinett* wines, when there should be few unripe grapes on any of the bunches. They are fuller and more complex than the *Kabinett* wines, should also be dry (with a fruitier aroma), and go well with food. They, too should be drunk within five years.
>
> *Auslese:* These wines are made from the latest picked

grapes before the mould needed to cause the grapes to shrivel up has appeared. Each bunch is examined, and all unripe grapes are discarded. They tend to be sweeter than the earlier picked wines, and may be served with dessert or with reasonably highly flavored foods. They should be drunk between four and seven years old.

*Beerenauslese:* These wines are made from overripe grapes, on which the mould is beginning to appear. They are quite sweet, with a very strong and fruity aroma and a powerful and long-lasting finish. They should be served with dessert and drunk between five and fifteen years old. They are usually quite expensive.

*Trockenbeerenauslese:* These wines are made from individual overripe grapes, which have been attacked by the mould to evaporate the water and to concentrate the essence of the grapes. They are the finest and most expensive German wines, and should be drunk on their own or with dessert. These wines (also the Beerenauslese wines) can be made only in the very best vintage years when the summer is long and warm. They age very well in the bottle and should be drunk between ten and twenty years old.

*Eiswein:* Sometimes the weather plays an unfair trick on the winemaker, and a sudden early frost strikes and freezes the grapes on the vine. In order to find a silver lining to this cloud, the winemaker crushes the grapes and makes a wine anyway.

Since this is somewhat rare, little of this wine is made, and it is sold at a premium. We have not found that it is good enough to justify the premium, and suggest that you spend your money elsewhere.

## The Producer

Apart from the very best, most German wines are blends from different estates, only some of which are owned by the producers. As a result, the vast majority of German wines available in the United States are made by a few independent producers. Therefore, you need be concerned with only a limited number of names.

Nevertheless, the skill, resources and diligence of the winemaker are still critical in the quality of the wine made. Even though the official classifications give a good indication of the overall quality of the wine, there are still variations between wines made by different producers.

These variations tend to be the same from year to year, since most producers buy the grapes from the same vineyards, year after year, and use the same production methods. The problem is to determine which producers make wines that you, personally, enjoy.

The solution is the same "try, taste, and test" that we recommend elsewhere. You need to try the wines of several producers until you find some who produce wines you like. If you like one wine from a particular producer, you will probably like others.

You don't know how sweet a particular winemaker makes his wine. Because the very best late-picked QmP wines are rather sweet, there is a tendency to think that if a German wine is sweet, it is a good wine. As a result, many German producers deliberately make their wines on the sweet side.

Some producers label their wines to tell you how dry it is. The terms used are *"Trocken"* (German for dry) and *"Halb Trocken"* (half dry—which is actually rather sweet). These terms are not required under the law; each producer can decide whether he wishes to use them.

Somes wines are sold under the *"Liebfraumilch"* (mother's milk) label. These are among the best-selling German wines in the United States, and many people think that it is a special type of wine.

However, all that this label tells you is that the wine is at least a QbA wine, and that it was made in the Rhine Valley. Most producers make a very reasonable wine under this label, but it rarely qualifies for the higher price often charged for it.

You can usually get a better German wine, for the same (or less), money by trying another QbA or even a QmP level wine, than you will get by buying a *Liebfraumilch*.

## *The Importer*

As with the wines of Bordeaux, there are certain houses that specialize in importing German wines. We have found that some firms consistently import wines that are good (or good value for the money), while wines imported by other firms have often been disappointing.

It may be the level of expertise is higher in those firms that consistently bring in good wines; alternatively, the taste of the importer may be similar to ours. In either case, we consistently like the wines of some importers, and not those of others.

We therefore suggest that you remember the names of the firms that have imported wines that you like, and use this to guide you when you are faced with a selection of unfamiliar German wines.

## *The Grape Varietals*

The three varietals most commonly used for German wines are the Riesling, the Sylvaner, and the Müller-Thurgau (a hybrid of the other two). All of the best German wines are made from the Riesling, (which is thriving in California, and doing reasonably well in New York state). The other varietals are used because they produce more wine than the Riesling, but it is of lower quality.

The producer has the option of putting the name of the varietal on the label, provided that at least 85% of the wine is made from it. In the past, the only wines to show the varietal were those that were made from the Riesling grape, since the others were deemed inferior. Today, almost all wines that are made from the Riesling will show it, but some producers are showing the names of the other grapes as well.

## The Vintage

Since most summers in Germany are rather cool, there are relatively few years that produce great wines. The quality classifications take this into account.

In poorer years, when the the producers add sugar to the grape juice, an acceptable wine can be made. In these years, the wines are almost always limited to the lower QbA quality level, but are still quite pleasant to drink.

In better years, no sugar is added, and the wines reach the QmP standards. The truly superior wines, made when the harvesting of the grapes can be delayed, can only be made in the very best years when the weather is especially favorable.

As a consumer, you can thus safely ignore the quality of any particular vintage, and simply use the year that the wine was made to ensure that you drink the wine at the right age. The classification system does the work for you!

## Designations of Origin

The producer will always use the best regional designation to which his wine is entitled. Although we do not feel that the region in which the wine was made makes a great deal of difference, the size of the classified area is important. The smaller the official designation of origin, the better should be the wine.

In the past, German wine labels were very confusing, and only the experts on German wines could determine where a particular wine came from. The recent German wine laws have simplified the labels considerably, and there are only four designations of origin to remember.

The largest designated region for a QbA (or better) wine is called a *"Gebiet,"* which is roughly similar to a French Region. The Mosel-Saar-Ruwer is a *Gebiet*, and wines carrying this label can be made from grapes grown in a number of estates in different communes within this region. This is similar to French wines labeled *Appellation Bordeaux Contrôlée*.

A smaller winegrowing commune within a *Gebiet* is called a *"Bereich"*. For example, Bernkastle is a *Bereich* within the Mosel-Saar-Ruwer *Gebiet*, and wines carrying this label will have been made from grapes grown within the boundaries of this commune. This is similar to a French wine labeled *Appellation Pauillac Contrôlée*. Some people argue that a *Bereich* is similar to a French District (e.g. Haut-Médoc), but we feel that they are too small for this classification.

The next designation is called a *"Grosslage,"* and is a collection of a few particularly good estates. There is no French equivalent.

The very best wines come from the few great *"Einzellagen,"* or classified estates. These can be identified by the price, and by the fact that the label merely shows the name of the estate (often using the word *"Schloss,"* which means castle), and the *Gebiet* (e.g. Rheingau).

They will always show the name of the producer (many of these estates have multiple owners, as in Burgundy, each of whom makes his own wine) and the words showing that the wine was Estate Bottled. They do not have to show the name of the commune, nor the grape varietal used (Riesling is assumed), and usually don't show either of these.

All Estate Bottled German wines carry the words *"Erzeuger Abfüllung,"* or *"Aus eigenem Lesegut"*. Not all Estate Bottled wines come from one of the classified estates. If the most prominent name on the label is the name of an estate, then you know that the wine is from one of the great classified estates.

If the most prominent name is that of the commune, "Bernkastle," for example, the wine is not from a classified *Einzellage*, but from a less prestigious estate within the commune. This is similar to the rules for French Burgundies.

## The Winemaking Regions of Germany

Although the differences among the official classifications are your best guide to which German wine you should drink, there are some subtle differences between the wines of the different regions.

*The Rhine Valley:* The official *Gebieten* of the Rhine are the Rheingau, Rheinhessen, Rheinpfalz, and the Mittelrhein, of which the first three are the best known.

The Rheingau is generally considered to be the best of the three, and is predominantly planted with the Riesling varietal. You will generally find that wines of the other three do not show a varietal label, since the producers do not wish to advertise the fact that most of these wines are made from the Sylvaner, although the best vineyards are also Riesling.

The Rhine wines are those most typically thought of as German wines. They are a golden yellow, with a very fruity aroma, taste and finish. The better wines are dry, although many, particularly those sold as *Liebfraumilch* tend to be rather sweet. The best late-picked wines come from this area, although there are also some good late-picked Mosel wines.

*The Mosel:* Wines from the Mosel and the rivers that flow into it, are all in the Mosel-Saar-Ruwer *Gebiet*. The Mosel river flows into the Rhine. The vineyards are farther north than those of the Rhine, with the result that the wines are somewhat lighter and less powerful than those of the Rhine.

Mosel wines are sold in long thin green bottles, as opposed to the brown bottles of the Rhine wines, and the color of the wine is lighter, usually with a touch of green. The taste and the aroma of the Riesling grape, which is the main varietal for Mosel wines, is as powerful as it is in the Rhine wines, but seems less complex and subtle.

*Franken:* Wines from Franken (Franconia) are not sold in the tall, thin bottles characteristic of Rhine and Mosel wines, but in short, fat bottles. They lack the finesse of the better-known Rhine wines, but are pleasant and inexpensive wines made from the Sylvaner varietal and are usually very good value.

*Other Regions:* The other officially designated winegrowing regions on the rivers of the Rhine are the Nahe, Baden and Neckar. These wines, which are not widely available in the United States, range from very good in the Naher, to generally less good in the other two. In addition, there is also the Bodensee region, near the Swiss border which makes a pale rosé wine from the Pinot Noir varietal.

# 12. The Wines of Italy

## Introduction

Italy produces more wine than any other country in the world. About two thirds of the production is red wine *(Rosso)*, and most of the rest is white *(Bianco)* although some rosé *(Rosato)* and sparkling *(Spumanti)* wines are also produced.

The Italians produce some of the finest wines in the world (particularly some of the full-bodied red wines), but they also produce some of the least good. Most of the best wines come from the more northerly parts of Italy, where the weather is cooler, but some quite reasonable wines are also made in the south.

Until recently, it was virtually impossible to select an Italian wine with any confidence at all, unless one happened to be a friend of the importer! The names of Italian wines, even the good ones, could refer to a grape varietal, a place, a family, a historical event, or even be made up entirely by the producer. Quality standards were erratic, and uncontrolled.

It would be nice to say that the *Denominazione di Origine Controllata* (usually abbreviated to DOC) decree passed in 1963 changed the situation at the stroke of a pen, and that the descriptions of Italian wines are now perfect.

Of course that did not happen, but it is safe to say that great progress has been made in the last 20 years, and one can now buy Italian wines with more confidence than ever before.

The decree, which was modeled after the French A.O.C. laws, requires that all good Italian wines carry the official DOC wording.

Some of the fanciful names are still used, which is unfortunate but understandable. However, most of the DOC wines use the name of the area, often with the predominant (and DOC required) varietal attached to the official name.

This book concentrates on the the wines of Italy that are readily available in the U.S., and the great wines of Italy that you can find if you look for them. We start with the DOC laws, and how you can use them to help you with all Italian wines.

## *Official Classifications*

*Denominazione di origine Controllata e Garantita* (DOCG):
Under the DOC decree, the Italian government foresaw the need to be able to classify certain wines as being really superior. This classification will be given to estates whose wines are truly superior to the normal DOC wines. This is similar to the French classified growth estates.

Only four regions have qualified for this classification. Since they are all full-bodied red wines, they must be aged in the barrel for several years before being bottled, and none is expected to be released before 1985.

We mention this classification, even though the the wines will not be seen for several years because they are already the giants of the Italian wine scene, both in terms of quality and price. They are well worth looking for.

In order for an estate to be granted a DOCG classification, the growers have to comply with very strict requirements, the production methods for the wine are controlled, and the wine itself will be tested and tasted. The bottles themselves will also have special seals to prevent any tampering with the wine.

These wines will probably reach the prestige (and prices) of the top classified estates in France, and it is worth laying some down if you have suitable storage facilities.

*Denominazione di Origine Controllata* (DOC): This is the official classification for the 15% of the entire Italian wine production that conforms to the legal requirements for superior wines. These requirements are similar to those for French and German classified wines and are as follows:

it is from the area named;
it was made from the specified varietal(s);
the maximum yield from the vineyard was not exceeded;
the wine was made from the grapes of the stated vintage year; and
the wine passed the chemical and taste tests.

*Vino Tipico:* This is the new classification for all the European Common Market countries; it is a step below the DOC wines and a step above the table wines. The requirements are similar to those for the DOC wines, but the controls are less strict. As a result they are good drinking wines, without any great distinction.

Although these wines are beginning to become available, many good DOC wines are little more expensive and give such good value for the money that it hardly seems worthwhile to spend a lot of time and effort on *Vini Tipici*.

We are told that both these wines and DOC wines will be entitled to use the letters "V.Q.P.R.D." (quality wine produced in the named region), which have recently been appearing on some Italian wines sold in the United States.

*Vino da Tavola* (Table wine): These are wines that do not

conform to the standards for any of the higher classifications. They may be made from any grape varietal, using virtually any methods the winemaker may choose.

The one guarantee that you have is that every wine exported from Italy, from the best DOCG to the least expensive Vino da Tavola, must carry the familiar red seal of the Italian Export Institute (INE). It is also important to check that the letters I.N.E. appear on the cork as well. This certifies that the contents of the bottle conform to the label, and that the wine is fit to drink.

We have found the quality standards for the classification of Italian wines to be the lowest in Europe, although they are improving. With some exceptions, Italian table wines that do not conform to the standards of any of the higher classifications are generally badly made.

However, this does not mean that you should dismiss all Italian table wines. Just to make life confusing, there are some producers of very fine wines who disagree with the Italian government, and who refuse to make their wines using, for example, the required grape varietals. These wines are then required to be called Vino da Tavola.

Since these wines are little known outside of the ranks of those who specialize in Italian wines, you will probably have difficulty in identifying these special cases. To be safe, we would suggest that you should generally avoid all wines that are classified as a Vino da Tavola.

After looking at the official classifications, there are some other words which may be on the label of the better DOC wines, and which can give you some more useful information.

*"Classico"* after the name of the wine (e.g. Valpolicella *Classico*) tells you that the wine was made in the center of the winegrowing district, and usually denotes a better level of quality.

In addition, many of the winegrowers in these districts have formed a local consortium whose members agree to maintain quality standards above the minimum DOC requirements. As a result, these wines are usually priced at a premium, which is usually worth paying.

These consortia have developed special seals that usually appear on the neck of the bottle and the presence of this seal is a very good indication that the wine will be above average. For example, the consortium of the best growers in the Chianti *Classico* district has adopted a seal with a black cockerel. Any Chianti *Classico* with this seal has conformed to the additional requirements of the consortium and should be pretty good.

There are too many consortia to list here, but these wines can usually be identified by the presence of a label on, or near, the neck of the bottle, with the word *"Consorzio"* somewhere on it.

The words *"Vecchio"* and *"Riserva"* may also appear on the label and are significant. They both mean that the wine has been aged in the barrel for a number of years before being bottled (*Riserva* is older than *Vecchio*). This improves the quality of full-bodied red wines and is only done for wines that the producer feels are superior.

These words can also give you an important clue about the type of wine itself. The DOC requirements allow the producers a considerable amount of latitude in the percentages of the permitted grape varietals that they may use in making a wine. In some cases, the differences can totally change the character of the wine between a full-bodied red wine, and a light red wine that is ready to drink at once.

If either word is present, you know that the wine is full-bodied and should be allowed to mature for some years before being drunk. If the words are not there, it is likely, although not absolutely certain, that it is a light red wine that should be drunk young.

Estate Bottled wines will carry the words *Imbottigliato* (or *Messo in bottiglia*) *nel'origine* (or *del produttore all'origine*). Other wines may try to fool those who do not speak Italian by saying that the wine was bottled *"nello stabilimento della ditta"* (on the premises of the firm!), or some other similar wording. The key word is *"origine"*.

## Producers and Importers

The reputation of the individual or firm that selects the grapes, and makes and bottles Italian wine is the single most important factor in selecting the wine. The same firm sometimes also imports and markets the wine in the United States.

Apart from some Estate Bottled wines, most Italian wines are relatively inexpensive, and there cannot be much profit on each bottle sold. As a result, the producers and importers seem to follow one of three strategies. The quality of the wine appears to be related to the strategy followed.

The first strategy is followed by the mass merchandisers, who use high powered (and expensive) marketing techniques to push their wines to the entire marketplace. These tend to be inferior table wines with little to recommend them.

The second tier consists of a relatively small number of producers and/or importers who are more restrained in their use of advertising. These firms, some of which are quite large, make or import DOC wines from one or more regions and are building their reputations on the basis of the consistent quality of their wines. These are usually the best Italian wines for the money, with the lowest risk of getting a poor wine.

The final tier consists of those producers and/or importers that specialize in the more exotic Italian wines, particularly the Estate Bottled wines. These include the very best Italian wines, but there are also some that have been very disappointing.

The probability of getting a decent wine from one of the

better DOC or DOCG districts is quite good, but it is almost impossible to come up with any good rules of thumb to guide you for Estate Bottled Italian wines. Our best suggestion is to put yourself in the hands of a wine store or restaurant that specializes in these wines, and try them on a case by case basis. If the proprietor really knows his stock, you will often get a truly superior wine at a very good price.

## Vintages

There is not generally a significant difference between the wines made in different years for most of the lighter Italian red wines and the white wines. Most Italian wines are blends of several grape varietals. The producers change the percentages of each varietal, to compensate for variations in the weather, and usually manage to produce wines that are relatively consistent from year to year. Since these wines should all be drunk within a few years of the harvest anyway, you can safely ignore the vintage year.

Even though the best full-bodied red wines come from the more northerly estates in Italy, these are still somewhat farther south than the major full-bodied red wine regions of France. Thus the weather is usually more consistent, and there are fewer years when the differences between vintages (*vendemmia*) are really significant.

We therefore suggest that, rather than trying to remember a host of numbers, you should use the year in which the wine was made as a guide to tell you when to drink the wine. With a few exceptions, the prices of mature full-bodied red Italian wines have not risen as much as that of the older French wines. You can thus buy mature *Vecchio* or *Riserva* wines at reasonable prices.

## The Winemaking Regions of Italy

In most major wine-producing countries, winegrowing is concentrated in locations favorable for the cultivation of vines. In Italy, wine is grown in every corner. In addition, many, many grape varietals are used, some of which produce the great wines of France and elsewhere, and some of which are unique to Italy.

*Piemonte:* The Piemonte region, in the northwestern corner, produces many of Italy's finest wines. The best known of the thirty-six DOC classified districts are Barbaresco, Barolo, and Asti-Spumanti. Many of the others combine the name of the varietal with the name of the place (e.g. the wines of Nebbiolo d'Alba; Nebbiolo is the grape, Alba the place).

Barolo and Barbaresco, both of which have recently been granted the DOCG classification, produce superb full-bodied red wines. We find these wines to be very similar, although many argue that the Barbaresco wines are somewhat lighter. Both are very powerful wines, and need to be aged for at least seven years before the tannin begins to soften. They will usually last for twenty or more years.

They both throw a heavy sediment, so they need to be decanted carefully, even when quite young. They are a very deep, purplish red and demonstrate the character of the Nebbiolo grape strongly in the aroma and taste. The finish is powerful, and lingers in the mouth long after the wine has been swallowed.

Asti Spumanti produces Italy's best known and best loved white sparkling wine. It is made from the Moscato (Muscat) grape varietal, which gives a heady, very fruity and powerful aroma and finish.

Its color is somewhat more golden than that of the French Champagnes, and it is almost always sweeter than the Brut Champagnes. For those who like their Champagnes on the sweet side, the better Asti Spumantis are almost as good, and considerably less expensive.

*Veneto:* Veneto, in the northeast of Italy, produces more wines for export than any other DOC region. The most commonly found wines in the United States are those from the DOC districts of Bardolino (red), Valpolicella (red), and Soave (white).

The red wines are both pleasant, light wines that are rarely complex, and are generally rather low in alcoholic content. They are rarely very expensive. Valpolicella is supposed to be somewhat darker and stronger than Bardolino, but we have found that this varies between different producers.

Soave is Italy's most exported white wine, and with good reason. It is rarely expensive, and is light and dry enough to go with most foods. A good Soave is a pale straw color, and has a fragrant aroma and a smooth, short-lived finish. It should be drunk very young, within two or three years, as should the red Bardolino and Valpolicella wines.

*Tuscany:* Tuscany, somewhat to the south of Piemonte, is the home of Italy's best known full-bodied red wine, Chianti, as well as the other two DOCG wines, Brunello di Montalcino and Vino Nobile di Montepulciano.

Chianti highlights the difficulties in drawing any wide conclusions about Italian wines, regardless of what may be on the label. It is made from a blend of grape varietals, and the producer may select the percentages of each, so long as at least 50% of the wine comes from one varietal, the Sangiovese.

Depending on how much of the softer Trebbiano grape is used, the wine may be a full-bodied red wine, harsh when young, or a fresh light wine, ready to drink at once.

In addition to the presence of the words *Riserva* and *Vecchio*, for full-bodied wines, the shape of the bottle for

Chianti wines can often give you a useful clue. If the wine comes in the same shaped bottle as wines from Bordeaux, with high, clearly defined shoulders, it is an indication that the wine is intended to be aged in the bottle, since this shape is convenient for storage.

If the Chianti comes in a magnum (1.5 litres, as opposed to the normal sized wine bottle, which is half as large), or in any other shaped bottle, the chances are good that it is intended to be drunk young. Sadly, Chianti is rarely found today in the bottles enclosed in straw baskets—they are too expensive to make and to ship. If you do find one, you know that the wine is ready to drink at once.

The wines from the center of the Chianti district are entitled to be called "Chianti *Classico*". They are usually the better Chiantis, and are intended to be aged in the bottle and drunk between five and about ten years old.

The wines of Brunello di Montalcino and Vino Nobile di Montepulciano are rated as the best of all the Italian wines, and are already very expensive. In a New York restaurant, we recently saw a bottle of Brunello priced at over one thousand dollars! They are both very powerful full-bodied red wines, that need ten years, or more, to mature.

The wines from these areas command very high prices, simply by virtue of the name. However, there are enormous variations in the quality of the wines from different estates, and the wines need to be approached on an estate by estate basis.

The risks in buying expensive wines from these areas will be reduced significantly once the DOCG ratings are granted only to the wines of the best estates. However, until then, we recommend that you do not fish in this pond without expert guidance.

*Umbria:* The most famous wine from the province of Umbria, to the east of Tuscany, is the white wine of Orvieto.

In Italy, the sweeter *(Abboccato)* wines are preferred, although a dry *(Secco)* version is also made, mainly for export.

Orvieto should be a deep golden color, and has a lush, very fruity aroma and taste. The finish is strong, and long lived. It should be drunk young, and makes a good aperitif, particularly the sweeter variety.

*Other Areas:* Italy produces many more wines than we can cover here. Among those that are reasonably available in the United States are the white Verdicchio and the red Lambrusco wines. Both of these are the names of grape varietals that are found in several DOC districts.

There are no failsafe rules for determining which of these wines will be good. Our suggestion is the same as that for exploring the Estate Bottled wines: you should find an establishment that specializes in Italian wines and follow the advice of the proprietor.

# 13. The Wines of the United States

*Introduction*

The United States is the newest of the major wine-producing countries, and is beginning to produce some of the finest wines in the world.

The industry, which was thriving in the last century, was devastated by the passing of Prohibition in 1920. During the thirteen years that Prohibition was in effect, most winemakers went bankrupt, and most of the vineyards were ruined or abandoned.

After Prohibition was repealed, the industry started up again, but American wine drinkers tended to be rather snobbish and would drink only fashionable European wines. Since there was no market for premium quality American wines, very few adventurous souls were willing or able to make the large investment necessary to start a premium winery.

As a result, only inexpensive jug wines were made, and these were generally of poor quality. To make things worse, the winemakers named these rather poor wines after the famous and respected premium wines of Europe.

Since these wines bore little resemblance to the wines they were named after, the prejudices of those who even tried American wines were confirmed. American wines gained a worldwide reputation for being inferior. The producers of

Bordeaux and the Rhine Valley slept soundly at night, unconcerned about competition from this side of the Atlantic.

Over the last fifteen years or so, a quiet revolution has taken place in the U.S. winemaking industry, and those same French and German producers are very wide awake indeed! Enormous amounts of capital and hard work have been invested in American vineyards and wineries, making them among the most modern and efficient in the world.

In addition, the expertise of the United States winemakers has grown enormously. The faculty and facilities for oenology at the University of California at Davis are now acknowledged as being the best in the world.

American wines are now winning major competitions around the world. Clearly this trend will continue, and it is no longer necessary to drink imported wines to get a superior wine.

At the present time, there are two major winegrowing areas in the United States—California and New York. Many more areas are now being planted with vines, but it takes five to ten years for a vine to produce good wine grapes. Therefore, little of this wine is available, and most is sold only in the area in which it was made.

## *Official "Classifications"*

The United States wine industry is regulated by the Bureau of Alcohol, Tobacco and Firearms (BATF). This agency has three main areas of concern, as far as wine is concerned.

The first is that the wine was properly made and is safe to drink. The second is that the contents of the bottle are clearly and honestly described on the label.

The last area is defining and enforcing standards showing the origins of the wine and granting special classifications to so called "Viticultural Areas" where the soil and climate are favorable for the production of superior wine. These are also areas where winemaking is flourishing, and the producers are willing to apply strict standards for the cultivation of the vines and the making of the wine.

The concept is similar to the French communal appellations, and the wines from these areas (e.g. Napa Valley) are already selling at a premium over similar wines from less prestigious locations.

It is still too early to tell whether the wines from these areas will consistently be superior. The soil and climate have been rated as superior, and the wines sell at a premium, so they certainly have every chance to maintain their quality.

Most are in California, although there are others in other states, including the first one ever to be designated, Augusta, in Missouri. These wines can be identified by the fact that they do not show the name of a state or a county on the label, merely the name of the officially designated area.

Some wines produced in these areas are made by the very large wine-producing corporations, and others by small wineries, often called "Boutique Wineries". If the wine is called "Estate Bottled" (or any wording implying the same thing), it means that all of the wine was made and grown on one estate. Quality levels can vary, depending on the skill, hard work and resources of the producer.

The next level of classification are wines that come from within a particular county (e.g. Sonoma County). This is only really important for Californian wines, where some winegrowing counties are so warm that they can only produce inexpensive jug wines while other counties have climates that are favorable for the growing of premium vines. The better counties are in northern California.

The next category of wines is those whose labels merely show the name of a state. Except for Californian wines this is the only classification that is frequently used, and may well be the best classification there is for the states that use it. We have not seen any New York state wines, even the best ones, that use the name of the county, rather than the name of the state.

If the label of a wine merely says that the wine is American, it may have been made anywhere in the United States, and is unlikely to be particularly good. If the grapes were grown in one of the better winegrowing states, the label would say so.

## *Grape Varietals*

In the countries with a long tradition of making wine, such as France, Germany and Italy, the name of the wine defines the grape varietal(s) used, even when the name of the varietal is not on the label. In order to maintain control over the quality and consistency of the wines using the regional name, only these grapes are permitted.

In the United States, any varietal can be grown in any location, and each producer is free to make wines from whatever varietals he wishes. In fact, many estates have different types of vines growing side by side.

All premium United States wines are varietal wines, and have the name of the varietal on the label. Before 1980, at least 50% of any wine showing the name of a varietal had to consist of the varietal named. Since then, the percentage has been increased to 75%, and there are discussions about increasing this to 100%.

This is very helpful to connoisseurs and beginners alike. An experienced consumer, who knows the grape varietals used in the European wines that he likes, can find similar American wines by selecting the same varietal.

For those who are just beginning to understand wine, there are only a few names to remember, and once these have been mastered, the foundation is built for exploring wines from around the world. This is why we suggest that you concentrate on just a few of the most common varietals.

There are two quite different types of grape families used to make wine in the United States. The first, which is native to the United States, is the "Vitis Labrusca" family (not to be confused with the Italian Lambrusco varietal).

The second is the "Vitis Vinifera" family which was imported from Europe and the Middle East, and from which all of the major European wines are made. All of the varietals mentioned so far in this book have been the Vinifera grapes.

Labrusca grapes can withstand harsh winters and are used for winemaking primarily in the northern states. The Vinifera grapes do not like the short summers and cold winters of New York, and are grown primarily in California.

The Labrusca grapes all impart to the wine a particular flavor (known as "foxy") which is very distinct in the finish, and is not widely liked. This is another reason why American wines had a poor reputation until recently, since the early American wines were all made from grapes of this family.

The origin of the word foxy has nothing to do with the small animal that is pursued on horseback by ladies and gentlemen in pink coats. Rather, it refers to the fox grape, which grows wild all over the country.

The most common Labrusca grape is the Concord, although you rarely see the name on the label. It is used primarily for inexpensive, and inferior, jug wines. It is also the primary grape for grape sodas and grape jelly.

Other, and better, Labrusca grapes that you may find are the Catawba, Delaware, Niagara and Duchess. Labrusca/Vinifera hybrids, which combine the hardiness of the Labrusca with a less foxy flavor, are also being developed. Some of the better known are the Aurora, Seyval Blanc and Rougeon varietals.

Red wines from the Labrusca grapes generally have an intensely foxy flavor, but the white wines are improving by leaps and bounds. This is true for both still and sparkling wines.

The Vinifera grapes that you will find most frequently are those which are used to make the most famous European wines, plus one, the Zinfandel which appears to be unique to the United States.

Since the soil and climate in the United States are different from those in Europe, the wines will never be exactly the same. Nevertheless, except for the Pinot Noir, which seems to thrive only on the Côte d'Or in Burgundy, Vinifera varietals produce wines on this side of the Atlantic that are similar to the European originals.

## *The Producer*

Wine producers are licensed before they may sell wine to the public. This provides you with some assurance that the wine has been properly made, and that the contents are as stated on the label.

Some producers use the old fashioned ways, and produce only limited quantities of wine, while others use massive modern production facilities to produce thousands of gallons per day. Some producers even use both methods for different types of wine.

As with the Italian wines, there seem to be three tiers of American firms who produce and market their wines.

The first tier consists of the large mass merchandising corporations who make enormous quantities of jug wines, often calling them "Chablis," "Burgundy," or some other respected name. These wines are sold as consumer products, backed by a very large advertising budget.

Some of these producers also make the so-called "Pop" wines (such as Cold Duck and others) which are sold under a variety of brand names. These may be still or sparkling, and are invariably rather sweet, additional sugar having been added after fermentation. These are usually blends of very poor wines, the sugar masking the imperfections in the quality.

Until recently, we would have recommended that you stay away from all the offerings of these mass merchandising corporations, which can be identified by the frequency of their commercials on television. However, some of them are also making high quality varietal wines which are winning major international competitions and offer good value for the money.

We suspect that these producers hope that their enhanced reputations will help them to increase the sales of jug wines. Nevertheless, we would still stay away from the jug wines and stick to the varietal wines.

The second tier consists of a small number of quite large wineries that specialize in high quality varietal wines. They have built their reputations on the quality of their wines rather than on the skill of their advertising agencies, and it is among these wines that you stand the best chance of finding the best American wines for the money.

These producers are large enough to make the investments necessary to maintain their facilities in top notch condition. At the same time, they are not so large that they have to peddle enormous quantities of wine to cover their overhead expenses.

They can be identified by the fact that the producer specializes in making varietal wines that are rarely, if ever, seen on television. Prices may be quite high, but are usually in the middle range of those for varietal wines. Some of these producers also make "house" wines, that are generally high quality blended wines, and are often excellent wines for the money.

A visit to one of these wineries is like visiting Bordeaux, Bernkastle, Piemonte and even Champagne, all at the same time. If you get the chance, they are well worth a visit. They are usually very hospitable, and will let you try their wares, generally without charge.

Most people, when they visit one of these wineries lose a

golden chance to advance their education in wine. They simply try each wine, without really using their heads to get the most out of the experience.

You need to keep your wits about you, which is admittedly rather difficult, and to pay close attention to the varietal, and to remember the type of European wine that is normally made from each one. In this way you can get a very good idea of all of the major wines, in one day and at no cost to you!

The final tier consists of the small wineries that produce some of America's finest wines, but also some of the nastiest wines that we have ever tasted. Some of these wineries, run by dedicated and skillful winemakers, are producing superb wines that are on a par with the best European estates.

If the producer is lazy, inexperienced or undercapitalized, the wine will generally be poor. This is not to say that poor wines are not also made by bad European winemakers, for they are. However, the A.O.C. and DOC regulations are more restrictive that U.S. laws on the permitted variations for the wine, so the problem is not as acute.

Most small estate wines are reasonably good, but it is impossible to judge this from the label. As with the wines from the smaller Italian producers, they have to be judged on an estate by estate basis. The only way to do this is to experiment with different wines, preferably with expert guidance.

## *The Wines of New York State*

New York is best known for its white wines, both still and sparkling, made from grapes of the indigenous Labrusca family. Most of the better wines are made in the Finger Lakes region, near Rochester and the Canadian border.

Some red wines are made either from the Labrusca or from the Vinifera grapes. Unfortunately, the summers are generally too short for the red grapes to ripen properly, and the winters are too harsh for the Vinifera vines to do well.

Some people like the foxy flavor from the Labrusca varietals, while others do not. Although the growers are trying to limit the taste, most New York wines have it, and it is entirely up to you to decide whether or not you like these wines.

The region is particularly famous for New York state Champagnes, usually made by the Champagne Method. Rather than use the words "Champagne Method" in English or French, the label will sometimes say that the wine was "Fermented in the Bottle," which means the same thing.

These wines, made from Labrusca grapes, lack the subtle elegance of French Champagnes, but the cork comes out of the bottle with the same satisfying pop, and the prices are much more reasonable. For most occasions, where snob value is not essential, they do just as well.

## *The Wines of California*

California has two distinct winegrowing regions, the northern part (east and north of San Francisco), and the central and southern part of the state. The northern part is known for the better quality varietal and table wines, while the southern part is better known for the fortified wines.

Most of California's especially designated viticultural areas are in the northern part. The most famous of these are the valleys of Napa, Santa Maria, Edna, San Pasqual, Guenoc, Alexander, McDowell, and Sonoma, plus the Santa Cruz Mountain viticultural area. In addition, Augusta (Missouri) and Fennville (Michigan) are also well known.

The California counties that are produce high quality wines are Napa, Sonoma and Mendocino, although we have also found superior wines carrying the labels of Monterey,

Santa Cruz and Santa Clara counties. Wines from any of these counties were made from grapes grown in a location which is favorable for producing superior wine.

The southern part of the state, the San Joaquin Valley, and an area near San Diego, generally produces fortified and inexpensive jug wines. Some success is being achieved with the Barbera and the newly developed Ruby Cabernet varietals.

## *Vintages*

*New York State:* Variations in the weather are less significant for white wines than for full-bodied red wines. In New York, as in many other places, when the weather has been poor, the producers are allowed to add sugar to the grape juice in order to produce a decent wine.

Although there are some differences between the white wines of New York produced in different years, we have found that these differences are not very pronounced, and are only of great interest to those who specialize in New York state wines.

*California:* California is blessed with the best, and most consistent, weather of any major winegrowing area in the world. There are very few truly awful years, most are good, and some are above average.

Our experience is that the skill of the producer far outweighs the quality of the vintage in the factors that should be considered in selecting a Californian wine. We suggest that you should simply use the vintage year as a guide to ensure that you do not drink a full-bodied red wine when it is too young, or any other wine when it is too old.

Many in the wine trade may disagree with some of our suggestions, such as our recommendation that you can safely ignore the vintage of a Californian wine. Others may disagree with our suggestions on the correct procedures for serving wines, such as our conclusion that it is proper to serve a white wine with steak, if that is what you like.

We stand behind these suggestions, which were developed over many years, in England, France, Germany, Italy and in the United States. They are the results of many successes, and some disappointments and we hope that you will be able to benefit from our experience, and avoid some of the mistakes that we have made over the years.

You now have an excellent knowledge of wine, far better than all but the professionals. You know enough to identify most of the situations where you are likely to get a bad bottle, and to return it with confidence if you happen to get one. You should never again be intimidated in a wine store or by the sommelier in a restaurant.

You know how to buy wine, how to store it, how to serve it elegantly and how to talk about it. In short, you can now hold your own in any company. Good luck, and Bon Appétit!

# Index

(Pronunciation of French Wines follow the names of the wines in parentheses.)

Acidity 62, 65, 68
Alcohol in wine 43
Alexander Valley 163
Aligoté (Al-ee-gohtay) 110
Alsace (Al-sass) 125, 126
Aloxe-Corton
   (Al-ox Kawr-tong) 116
Anjou (Ahn-jew) 18, 127
Appearance 61, 65
*Appellation (d'Origine) Contrôlée*
   (A.O.C) 89-92
      -Bordeaux 100-101
      -Burgundy 111-113
      -Champagne 121-122
Aroma 9, 61, 65, 67
Asti Spumanti 18, 68, 150
Astringency 65, 68
Augusta 163
Aurora 159
Auslese 17, 84, 135-136
Auxey-Duresses
   (Awk-see Doo-ress) 116

Baden 142
Barolo 14, 25, 150
Barbaresco 25, 150
Barbera 25, 164
Bardolino 16, 82, 84, 151
Barsac (Bar-zak) 97, 106

Beaujolais
   (Boh-zho-lay) 16, 107-117
   -*Cru Beaujolais* 113
   -*Nouveau* (Noo-voh) 113
   -*Supérieur* (Soo-pair-ee-er) 113
   -*Villages* (Vee-lahge) 113
Beaune (Bay-own) 116
Beerenauslese 136
Bereich 140
Bernkastle 140
*Blanc de Blancs* 17, 120
Blaye (Blay) 106
Bodensee 142
Body 65, 69
Bordeaux (Bor-doh) 23, 95-106
Bouquet 9, 67
Bourg (Bourg) 106
Breathing 42, 62
Brouilly (Bree-yee) 117
Brunello di Montalcino 151
Bureau of Alcohol, Tobacco and
   Firearms 156
Burgundy (French) 14, 23, 24,
   107-117
   -Other "Burgundies" 56, 160

Cabernet Sauvignon
   (Ka-ber-nay Soh-vee-nyong)
   14, 23, 24, 96, 97

Cabernet Franc (Ka-ber-nay frong) 97, 127
Catawba 85, 159
Cérons (Sair-oh) 106
Chablis (Shablee) 24, 56, 83, 107-116
Chambolle-Musigny (Shom-bol Moo-see-nyee) 116
Champagne (Sham-pain) 18, 68, 119-124
  -Glasses 36
  -Method 19, 122, 163
  -*Tête de Cuvée* 124
Chaptalization 21
Chardonnay (Shar-doh-nay) 16, 23, 24, 56, 108-110, 120
Character of wine 9
Chassagne-Montrachet (Sha-sine Mon-trash-ay) 116
Châteauneuf-du-Pape (Shatoh-nufdoo pup) 129
Château Haut Brion (Shatoh Oat Bree-ong) 103
Château Lafite (Shatoh La-feet) 103
Château Latour (Shatoh La-toor) 103
Château Margaux (Shatoh Mar-goh) 103
Château d'Yquem (Shatoh Dee-kem) 103
Chénas (Shay-na) 117
Chenin Blanc (Shey-nong blong) 25, 84, 127
Chianti 151-152
Chiroubles (Shee-roo-bleh) 117
Claret 95
Classico 146
Classified Estates 102, 111
Color 61, 66
Communal appellation 91, 101, 111

Corks - removing 38-41
  -Information on 60
  -Deteriorated (corked wine) 60
Corkscrews 37
Corton (Kawr-tong) 116
Côte-de-Brouilly (Coat duh Bree-yee) 117
Côtes-du-Rhône (Coat-doo-roan) 129
Côte Rôtie (Coat Roh-tee) 129

Decanting wines 41-43
  -in a restaurant 43
Delaware 159
Denominazione di Originata Controllata (D.O.C.) 143-145
  -e Garantita (D.O.C.G.) 144
Designation of Origin 12-13
Dinner (important) 47
Dry wines 15
Dry white wines 16, 25
Duchess 84, 159

Echézeaux (Ay-she-zoh) 116
Edna Valley 163
Einzellage 140-141
Eiswein 136
Enemies of (stored) wine 28
Entre-deux-Mers (Ehntruh-deh-mair) 106
Estate Bottled 58
  -France 100, 114, 125-126
  -Germany 141
  -Italy 147
  -U.S.A 157
Evaluation 63-71
  -Scoring 64-65, 78, 80

Fashion 75
Fennville 163

## Index

Fermentation 20, 21
   -in the bottle 163
Finger Lakes 162
Fining 21
Finish 9, 63, 65, 70
Fixin (Feek-sung) 116
Flavor 65, 69
Fleurie (Fler-ee) 117
Food and wine 33-34, 49
Fortified wines 19, 22, 33, 44
Foxy 159, 163
Franken 142
Fraud 54, 60
Fronsac (Frong-zak) 106
Full-bodied red wines 14, 25

Gamay (Ga-may) 25, 110
Gamay-Beaujolais 110
Gebiet 140
Gevrey-Chambertin (zhevray Shahm-bair-tahn) 116
Gewürztraminer 125, 126
Givry (zhee-vree) 116
Glasses 35
Grape Varietal, importance of 23
Graves (Grahve) 52, 106
Grenache (Greh-nash) 18, 25, 130
Grosslage 140
Guenoc Valley 163

Halb Trocken 137
Haut-Médoc (Oat May-dock) 85, 91, 106
Hermitage (Air-mee-tahj) 129
How wine is made 20-23
Humidity 28, 30

Intimidating the sommelier (wine waiter) 8, 50, 52, 165
Investing in wine 48

Juliénas (zhew-lee-ay-na) 117

Kabinett 135

Labels, information on 55-58
   -looking at 74
Labrusca (Vitis) 158-160, 163
Lambrusco 153
Landwein 133
Late-picked sweet white wines 17, 97-98
Liebfraumilch 137-138
Light red wines 16
Lirac (Lee-rak) 129
Listrac (Lee-Strak) 106
Loire (Lwahr) 126-128
Loupiac (Loo-pee-ak) 106

Margaux (Mar-goh) 90, 106
McDowell Valley 163
Médoc (May-dok) 53, 106
Mendocino County 163
Mercurey (Mair-cure-ay) 116
Merlot (Mair-loh) 85, 97
Méthode Champenoise (May-todd Shahm-pen-wahse) 19, 122-123
Meursault (Mare-soh) 116
Mittelrhein 141
Montagny (Mon-tan-yee) 116
Monterey County 163
Morey-St.-Denis (More-ay Sun Duhnee) 116
Morgon (More-Gong) 117
Moulin-à-Vent (Moo-lung ah Vong) 117
Mosel-Saar-Ruwer 140, 142
Mosel wines 16, 131-142
Moulis (Moo-lease) 106
Müller-Thurgau 138
Muscadet (Muss-ka-day) 127-128
Must 20

Nahe 142
Names of Wines 12-13

Napa County 163
Napa Valley 163
Néac (Nay-ak) 106
Nebbiolo 25, 150
   -d'Alba 150
Neckar 142
Nuits-St.-Georges
   (Nwee Suhn Jawj) 116

Opening wines 36-41
Order of drinking 77
Orvieto 152
Over the hill 28, 62, 67

Parties (Choosing wines) 36, 48-50
Pasteurizing wine 22
Pauillac (Poy-ak) 91, 106
Pernand-Vergelesses (Pair-nahn
   Vair-jay-less) 116
Pink Champagne 120
Pinot Chardonnay,
   see Chardonnay
Pinot Noir (Pea-noe nwahr)
   13, 25, 108, 109, 120, 160
Pommard (Poe-mar) 116
Pomerol (Pom-mair-oll) 102, 106
"Pop" wines 17, 22, 160
Port 20, 28
Pouilly-Fuissé
   (Pwee-yee Fwee-say) 116
Pouilly-Fumé
   (Pwee-yee foomay) 127
Pouilly-Loché
   (Pwee-yee Loh-shay) 116
Pouilly-Vinzelles
   (Pwee-yee Vun-zel) 116
*Pourriture Noble* 98
Prémeaux (Pray-moh) 116
Producer 9
Professional Caterers 36, 49, 50
Prohibition 155

Pronunciation of wine names 52
Prüfungsnummer 133, 134
Puligny-Montrachet
   (Poo-lee-nyee Mon-trashay) 116

Qualitätswein (bestimmter
   Anbaugebiete) 134
   -mit Prädikat 134

Restaurants, ordering wine in
   50-55
Returning a bad wine 46, 47, 48
Rheingau 140, 141
Rheinhessen 141
Rheinpfalz 141
Rhine wines 16, 28, 131-142
Riesling (Rhee-sling) 25, 125, 131
Riserva 147
Rosé (Roh-say) 18, 25
Rougeon (Roo-jay-ong) 159
Ruby Cabernet 164
Rully (Roo-yee) 116

San Joaquin Valley 164
San Pasqual Valley 163
Santa Clara County 164
Santa Cruz County 164
Santa Cruz Mountain 163
Santa Maria Valley 163
Saint Amour (Sunt-Amoor) 117
Saint Emilion
   (Sun tay-mee-yawn) 97, 106
Saint Estèphe (Sun tay-stef) 106
Saint Foy (Sun Fwa) 106
Saint Julien (Sun Joo-lee-yen) 106
Saint Macaire (Sun Ma-kair) 106
Saint Véran (Sun Vair-ahn) 116
Sainte Croix-du-Mont
   (Sunt Kwah-doo-moh) 106
Sancerre (Sun-sair) 127
Santenay (Sun-ten-ay) 116

Saumur (Soh-muir) 127
Sauterne (California) 98
Sauternes (Soh-tearn)
  17, 25, 28, 84, 94, 97, 106
Sauvignon Blanc (Soh-vee-nyawn Blong) 25, 82, 96-97, 127
Savigny (Sa-vee-nyee) 116
Scorecards 78, 80
Sediment 28, 65-66
  -decanting 41-42
Sekt 18, 83, 131
Semillon (Say-mee-yong) 25, 82, 97
Seyval Blanc 159
Sherry 20, 34
Soave 16, 82, 84, 151
Sonoma County 163
Sonoma Valley 163
Sparkling wines 18, 107, 131, 143
Spätlese 84, 135
Storage of Wine 27-31
  -acceptable 30
  -ideal 28
Sulfur dioxide 21
Sweet wines 17, 22
Sweetness 65, 68
Sylvaner 84, 125, 138
Syrah (See-rah) 129

Tafelwein 133
Tank method 19
Tannin 14, 15, 18, 27, 68
Tasting wine 61
  -A Wine Tasting 76-78
  --Introductory 82
  -Intermediate 83
  -Advanced 85
  -Horizontal 86
  -Vertical 85
  -Specialized 86
Tavel (Ta-velle) 25, 83, 128, 129, 130

Temperature - storage 28, 29
  -serving wines 34-35, 44
Touraine (Too-rain) 127
Trocken 137
Trockenbeerenauslese 136

Valpolicella 16, 82, 84, 151
Value of Wine Labeling Laws 88
Vayres (Vayer) 106
Vecchio 147
Verdicchio 153
Vermouth 20, 34
Vin Délimité de Qualité Supérieure 93
Vin de Pays 93
Vin de Table (Vin Ordinaire) 94
Vinegar 29, 60, 62, 65, 67
Vinifera (Vitis) 159, 163
Vino da Tavola 145-146
Vino Nobile di Montepulciano 151
Vino Tipico 145
Vintages 31-33
  -Bordeaux 98-100
  -Burgundy 110-111
  -Champagne 121
  -Germany 139
  -Italy 149
  -Rhône 129
  -U.S.A. 164-165
Viré(vee-ray) 116
Visiting a Winery 161
Viticultural Areas (U.S) 157, 163
Vosne-Romanée (Voan Roh-ma-nay) 116
Vougeot (Voo-jay-oh) 116
Vouvray (Voo-vray) 127

Weddings 36, 48-50
Wine Appreciation course 82-86

Zinfandel 25, 82, 85, 160

The PRACTICAL GUIDE TO WINE makes a perfect gift for graduations, weddings, showers, birthdays or Christmas. Why not give a copy to your family or friends?

To order, simply fill out the form below, and mail it with your check or Credit Card information to:

PRACTICAL PUBLISHING CORPORATION
POST OFFICE BOX 1020
LENOX HILL STATION
NEW YORK, N.Y. 10021

Prices (plus tax and $1.25 per copy Postage and Packing)

| Hardcover | $11.95 |
| Paperback | $6.95 |

Please send ___ Copies of the PRACTICAL GUIDE TO WINE.

Name _____

Address (Street) _____

City_____ State_____ Zip____

Credit Card  Visa ____  Master Charge ____

Account No._____ Expires ____/__

Signature _____

The PRACTICAL GUIDE TO WINE makes a perfect gift for graduations, weddings, showers, birthdays or Christmas. Why not give a copy to your family or friends?

To order, simply fill out the form below, and mail it with your check or Credit Card information to:

PRACTICAL PUBLISHING CORPORATION<br>
POST OFFICE BOX 1020<br>
LENOX HILL STATION<br>
NEW YORK, N.Y. 10021

Prices (plus tax and $1.25 per copy Postage and Packing)

    Hardcover        $11.95
    Paperback        $6.95

Please send ___ Copies of the PRACTICAL GUIDE TO WINE.

Name _____

Address (Street) _____

City_____ State_____ Zip_____

Credit Card   Visa _____   Master Charge _____

Account No._____ Expires _____/____

Signature _____